Chinese Folktales and Legends

An Enthralling Collection of Stories, Heroes, Magical Creatures, and Timeless Tales from Ancient China

© Copyright 2025 - All rights reserved.

The content contained within this book may not be reproduced, duplicated, or transmitted without direct written permission from the author or the publisher.

Under no circumstances will any blame or legal responsibility be held against the publisher, or author, for any damages, reparation, or monetary loss due to the information contained within this book, either directly or indirectly.

Legal Notice:

This book is copyright protected. It is only for personal use. You cannot amend, distribute, sell, use, quote, or paraphrase any part, or the content within this book, without the consent of the author or publisher.

Disclaimer Notice:

Please note the information contained within this document is for educational and entertainment purposes only. All effort has been executed to present accurate, up-to-date, reliable, and complete information. No warranties of any kind are declared or implied. Readers acknowledge that the author is not engaging in the rendering of legal, financial, medical, or professional advice. The content within this book has been derived from various sources. Please consult a licensed professional before attempting any techniques outlined in this book.

By reading this document, the reader agrees that under no circumstances is the author responsible for any losses, direct or indirect, that are incurred as a result of the use of the information contained within this document, including, but not limited to, errors, omissions, or inaccuracies.

Free limited time bonus

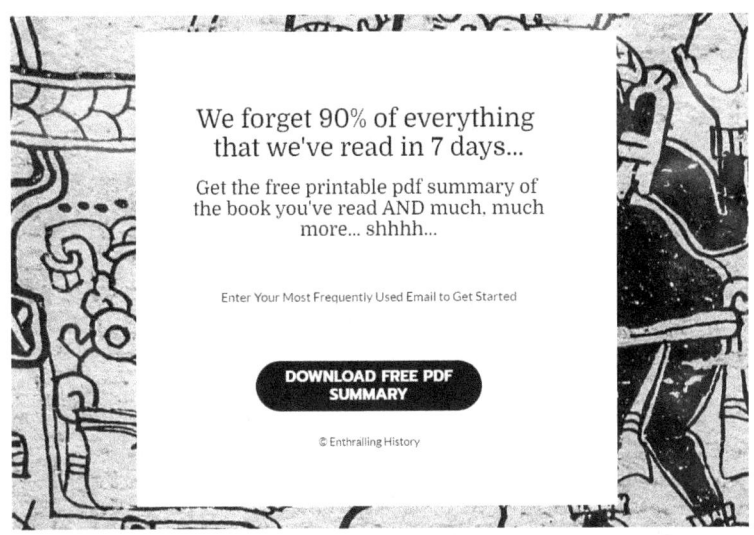

Stop for a moment. We have a free bonus set up for you. The problem is this: we forget 90% of everything that we read after 7 days. Crazy fact, right? Here's the solution: we've created a printable, 1-page pdf summary for this book that you're reading now. All you have to do to get your free pdf summary is to go to the following website:
https://livetolearn.lpages.co/enthrallinghistory/

Or, Scan the QR code!

Once you do, it will be intuitive. Enjoy, and thank you!

Table of Contents

HOW TO PRONOUNCE PINYIN 1
INTRODUCTION 2
CHAPTER 1: CHINA'S FOLKLORIC FOUNDATIONS 4
CHAPTER 2: THE JADE EMPEROR'S REALM 12
CHAPTER 3: LEGENDS FROM THE SILK ROAD 22
CHAPTER 4: TALES OF THE LOTUS POND 32
CHAPTER 5: THE GIFT OF THE DRAGON 42
CHAPTER 6: BAMBOO AND ITS SIGNIFICANCE 53
CHAPTER 7: PHOENIX LEGENDS 63
CHAPTER 8: WARRIORS OF DESTINY 71
CHAPTER 9: MOUNTAINS AND RIVERS: MAGICAL LANDSCAPES 79
CHAPTER 10: MAGICAL LANTERNS AND CHINESE FESTIVALS 88
CONCLUSION 96
HERE'S ANOTHER BOOK BY ENTHRALLING HISTORY THAT YOU MIGHT LIKE 98
FREE LIMITED TIME BONUS 99
BIBLIOGRAPHY 100
IMAGE SOURCES 102

How to Pronounce Pinyin

"Pinyin" means "spelled sounds." Chinese children spend years learning Chinese characters, but pinyin spells out the sounds in Chinese words phonetically. Learning the basics of pinyin will enable you to read the Chinese words in this book. (We will not worry about tone marks.)

Consonants

The consonants b, d, f, g, h, j, k, l, m, n, p, and t are pronounced like they are in English. Here is a basic guide to the other consonant sounds:

"j" sounds like the "j" in "jet"

"q" has a "ch" sound, so the word "Qin" sounds like "cheen"

"x" has an "sh" sound, so "Xian" sounds like "Shee ahn"

"zh" has a "j" sound with a flat tongue

"ch" is like the English "ch" but with a flat tongue

"sh" is like the English "sh" but with a flat tongue

"r" is like the English "r" but the tongue curls slightly back

"z" sounds like the "ds" in "birds"

"c" sounds like the "ts" sound in "bats"

"s" sounds like the "s" in "sun"

Vowels

"a" is like the "ah" sound in "father"

"o" sounds like the "oh" sound in "go"

"e" sounds like the short "e" in "pen"

"i" sounds like the long "e" in "see" (the word "Pinyin" sounds like peen yeen)

"u" sounds like the "oo" sound in "food"

Introduction

"Yeye! Yeye! Tell us a story! Please?"

The grandfather sat on his stool and lit his cigarette as the cousins pulled their stools close to him in the courtyard. The older children held the toddlers on their laps as evening approached. Behind them, the adults cleared the tables and squatted to wash dishes in basins on the courtyard floor. It was Chūnjié, the Chinese New Year, also known as Spring Festival. The extended family had gathered to celebrate in the ancestral village, as they had done for centuries. The grown-ups smiled as they glanced at the grandfather, surrounded by the children. Sharing their folklore was an essential element of their festivals.

"And what story shall I tell you, dear children?"

"Sun Wukong! Monkey King! Monkey King!" the children squealed.

"Monkey King? It's always Monkey King! I told you a Monkey King story yesterday and the day before! Tonight, I shall tell a different story that took place long before the Monkey King. It is the story of Pangu, who formed the universe, and Nuwa, who created people and repaired the sky."

"Was the sky broken?" asked a child.

"Yes, it was. And tonight, you'll learn what happened."

Just as Chinese grandparents have shared their legends for millennia, this book immerses readers in the rich tapestry of ancient China's myths and folklore. It vividly brings the enchanting tales of heroes and magical creatures to life. These ancient stories highlight the cultural, spiritual, and historical depth of Chinese traditions. They are not simply fairy tales; in fact, most dive into China's ancient history, where real people and events gained mythical status. The challenge is separating myth from reality.

These folktales introduce readers to Chinese insights and proverbs. China's people believe their history and mythology hold valuable life lessons and universal wisdom. Even today, their speech is full of idioms and catchphrases from these tales. Readers will enjoy the linguistic cleverness of these ancient stories through puns and other wordplay. Typical Chinese self-deprecating humor, subtle irony, witty dialogue, and layered meanings shine through these legends that readers of all ages can enjoy.

This book organizes Chinese folklore thematically into ten chapters, introducing key Chinese concepts such as yin and yang, the five elements, the phoenix, and the symbolism of the lotus. It brings characters like the Jade Emperor, the Monkey King, and the Dragon King to life. Readers will meet quasi-historical characters, such as Yu the Engineer, who introduced effective flood control measures and became the first emperor of the Xia dynasty. Magic, adventure, dashed hopes, realized dreams, and so much more await the reader in the coming chapters.

Chapter 1:
China's Folkloric Foundations

This chapter delves into the foundational myths and legends that lay the groundwork for China's rich folklore tradition. These stories offer invaluable insight into how the ancient Chinese perceived cosmic order and the world's origins. For instance, how did they think the universe and humanity came into being? Who established the world's natural and moral order? As we discuss these myths, remember that the Chinese had multiple versions of the stories.

How did the universe begin? According to Chinese mythology, before time began, nothing existed but a dark, chaotic void. The swirling chaos formed an egg, which contained the entire universe within a tiny space. It also held yin and yang: the opposite yet interconnected forces of balance and duality. Yang represents day, brightness, movement, and height (as in a mountain), while yin represents night, darkness, rest, and a closed door. Within the egg, yin and yang struggled against each other. Ultimately, they achieved balance for the first time, forming a hairy, horned, rotund dwarf named Pangu.

Pangu carried a giant axe, which he cracked the egg. As Pangu broke out of the egg, the universe also broke free. Pangu swung his axe, separating yin and yang, creating the Earth and sky. He stood on the Earth and held up the sky, which gradually rose higher as the Earth grew thicker. The longer Pangu held up the sky, the taller he grew, until he became a mighty giant.

The presence of Shangdi, China's supreme deity, is implied in the formation of the primeval egg. His name means "primordial, first, and highest." He was the ultimate great power, ruling over a hierarchy of other gods who emerged later in Chinese mythology. Shangdi transcended the material universe and physical laws.

At the Border Sacrifice, the emperor sacrificed a sheep or bull to Shangdi while reciting the following:

> "Of old, in the beginning, there was the great chaos, without form and dark. The five elements [planets] had not begun to revolve, nor the sun and moon to shine. You, O Spiritual Sovereign, first divided the grosser parts from the purer. You made Heaven. You made Earth. You made man. All things with their reproducing power got their being."[i]

The ancient Chinese believed that when their kings died, their souls merged with the supreme deity, Shangdi. Thus, the Chinese worshipped their ancestral kings, asking them to mediate with Shangdi. They believed Heaven (Tian) and Shangdi were essentially the same. Heaven was not so much a place as an abstract, cosmic force. The Chinese philosopher Mozi (408-382 BCE), who founded the Mohist school of thought, said this about Tian (or Shangdi):

> "I know Heaven (Tian) loves men dearly, not without reason. Heaven ordered the sun, the moon, and the stars to enlighten and guide them. Heaven ordained the four seasons, Spring, Autumn, Winter, and Summer, to regulate them. Heaven sent down snow, frost, rain, and dew to grow the five grains, flax, and silk so that the people could use and enjoy them. Heaven established the hills, rivers, ravines, and valleys, and arranged many things to minister to man's good or bring him evil."[ii]

Once Pangu hatched, divine creatures known as the "Four Benevolent Animals" arrived to assist him. They were the Dragon, Phoenix, Qilin, and Turtle. We will discuss the Dragon and the Phoenix in chapters five and seven. Together, these four creatures represented the Chinese constellations.

---

[i] James Legge, *The Notions of the Chinese Concerning Gods and Spirits* (Hong Kong Register, 1852), 28.

[ii] *The Works of Motze*, (Confucius Publishing Co., 1980), 290.

Artwork of the Turtle, or Black Tortoise, often shows a snake coiled around it. It was the "Black Warrior of the North." The Qilin had the body of a fiery horse (or goat) with cloven hooves and the head and tail of a dragon. It symbolized prosperity and good luck. When the Qilin appeared, it was an omen of the birth or death of a sage or an exceptional ruler.

The Qilin [1]

Eventually, Pangu died, and his body became the four pillars that supported the sky. By this time, other gods and goddesses had emerged. The Chinese believed certain mortals became gods after death, and Pangu was among those. They thought their deities lived in palaces on sacred mountains. One ancient deity was Gonggong, the water god. He had red hair, a human face, and a snake's body. Zhurong was the god of fire, yet he was known for doing nothing and desiring nothing. However, one day, he did do something.

Gonggong wanted to usurp the throne of Heaven and rule the cosmos. Zhurong sprang into action to stop him. The two gods clashed in a ferocious, protracted war, fighting in both Heaven and Earth. Zhurong finally won the battle, preserving Heaven's order. Gonggong was furious. He smashed his head against Mount Buzhou, one of the four pillars that held up the sky. When the sky collapsed, it opened Heaven's flood gates, and the Great Flood ensued.

Ancient China had two variations of when the Great Flood happened. Some accounts say it was a universal flood that occurred shortly after the world's creation. Other stories say it was a localized but horrific and prolonged flooding of the river system between the Yellow River and the Yangtze at the beginning of the Xia dynasty. In both cases, Gonggong was to blame. Chapter five will cover the second version, in which Yu the Engineer saved the day. This chapter unwraps the first version.

After Pangu died, his body not only formed the four pillars that hold up the sky (the four great mountains), but also gave rise to the rivers, plants, and animals. Huaxu was a goddess who emerged from Pangu's body. After stepping into a footprint of Lei Shen, the thunder god, Huaxu became pregnant and gave birth to Fuxi and his sister, Nuwa. Like their mother, the twins had human heads and serpent bodies. When Gonggong caused the Great Flood, Nuwa collected five colored stones from the river, melted them, and repaired the broken sky.

However, Fuxi and Nuwa were the only creatures that survived the flood. Fuxi turned to Nuwa. "We need to marry and repopulate the earth," he said.

"We can't marry!" Nuwa replied. "You're my brother!"

"Okay. We'll let Heaven decide. You climb that mountain, and I'll climb this one. Each of us will light a fire. If the smoke rises straight up, that means we should not get married. But if the smoke from my fire travels toward your mountain and the smoke from your fire comes out to meet it, that means that Heaven approves our marriage."

The smoke from the two fires merged, so the twins married and repopulated the earth. However, they did not do it in the usual way. With Fuxi's assistance, Nuwa created animals. On day one, she made chickens. The next day, she created dogs. On the third day, she made sheep, and on the fourth,

A Tang dynasty painting of Nuwa and Fuxi¹

7

pigs. She made cows on the fifth day and horses on the sixth. Finally, on the seventh day, Nuwa took yellow clay and formed two creatures with faces that resembled hers and Fuxi's: a man and a woman. She gave all her creations the ability to reproduce.

After people had lived on the earth for many years, they formed tribes that often fought each other for power. Huangdi (Yellow Emperor), China's legendary first emperor, was one of the "Five Great Emperors" of China. Chinese history claims he ruled a group of tribes from 2679 to 2597 BCE in north-central China. Written history that has survived to modern times does not mention him until the early fourth century BCE. However, the Chinese did not begin writing until about 1,400 years after the Yellow Emperor's reign. Although he probably was a real person, all the exploits attributed to him place Huangdi in legendary status. By the Han dynasty (which began in 202 BCE), followers of the Taoist religion worshipped him as a god.

The Yellow Emperor's given name was Xuan Yuan. Legend says that when he was conceived, a loud thunderclap rang out even though it was a clear day. As a young man, Huangdi was a farmer who learned to tame animals, like the bear and tiger. He taught his followers to build houses, grow grains, domesticate animals, make clothing, and sail in boats. (The ancient Mesopotamians had been doing all those things for at least two millennia.) Huangdi supposedly invented wheeled carts, but, once again, the Sumerians of southern Mesopotamia (Iraq) were already using chariots in his lifetime. He might have introduced these things to China, but Huangdi was not their first inventor.

Huangdi's path to becoming an emperor over multiple tribes began when he was the leader of the Youxiong (Bear) tribe, which warred against the Shennong (Bull) tribe. After the Youxiong tribe won, the two tribes united under the leadership of Huangdi, marking the beginning of Chinese civilization. However, a superhuman tribe, led by Chi You, challenged Huangdi's people. Chi You and his eighty-one brothers each had four eyes and eight arms. Huangdi formed a coalition with eight nearby tribes, yet the ensuing battle dragged on for days, with neither side taking the lead.

Huangdi's forces finally got the upper hand, but Chi You puffed a thick fog from his nostrils that blocked the sun. No one could see anything. In a panic, Huangdi's army tried to leave the battlefield but wandered around aimlessly in the mist. Just in time, Huangdi invented the "south-pointing" chariot, building it right there on the field despite the fog obscuring everything. The chariot's mechanisms pointed south, so he led his men away from the battle. Yet, before Huangdi and his me made their escape, Chi You used his black magic to call up a fierce storm. Huangdi prayed to the gods, and they dispersed the storm, enabling Huangdi to triumph over Chi You and his diabolical tribe.

What was the south-pointing chariot? It was a real thing, but Huangdi did not invent it. Horses and chariots did not appear in China until the Shang dynasty (1600-1046 BCE). An engineer named Ma Jun is credited with inventing the south-pointing chariot in the third century BCE. It was a two-wheeled chariot with gear and track ratios and a specific wheel size, which always kept a figure attached to the wheels pointing south. The south-pointing chariot was well-documented in Chinese histories, with detailed descriptions of its mechanics.

According to later tales, the Yellow Emperor was a sage who accomplished an incredible number of inventions. He reportedly developed traditional Chinese medicine, and it worked so well for him that he lived to be a hundred years old. He supposedly wrote China's first medical book; however, writing did not emerge in China until the Shang dynasty (1600-1046 BCE). Other innovations that legend says Huangdi introduced include the Chinese calendar, advanced mathematics, Chinese astronomy, coins, and China's first law code.

The Huangdi Temple in Xinzheng City, Henan Province [8]

Tradition also says the Yellow Emperor invented Cuju, a Chinese ball game that blended elements from today's soccer and basketball. Cuju was the world's first kicking game. The teams had to keep the ball in the air without touching it with their hands and kick it through a hoop in the center of the court. Intriguingly, the ancient Olmecs and other Mesoamerican tribes had an almost identical game, which the Aztecs called Ulama.

Taoism, a philosophical and religious system that developed in the sixth century BCE, elevated Huangdi to a deity. Taoists credited him with establishing the natural and moral order of the world by bringing harmony between Earth and Heaven. He achieved this by uniting the tribes to defeat the Chi You tribe, bringing peace and eliminating evil. Huangdi exemplified the core Chinese principles of harmony, cohesion, and respect for authority. The Chinese considered him the ideal ruler, who led with virtue, wisdom, moral integrity, and a keen understanding of natural law.

Taoists said he balanced "Wuxing," the Five Elements (wood, fire, earth, metal, water) that explain the universe's relationships and interactions. Each element is associated with specific parts of the body, influencing Chinese traditional medicine.

The first element, wood, represents new beginnings, growth, and flexibility. Springtime and the color green are associated with this element. The body parts connected to the element of wood are the gallbladder and liver. The second element, fire, represents energy and passion. Summer and the color red are linked to this element. Its body parts are the heart and the small intestine.

Earth is the third element, symbolizing nurture, stability, and practicality. It is connected to late summer and the color yellow. The pancreas, spleen, and stomach are the body parts associated with Earth. The fourth element is metal, representing structure, strength, and order. It is associated with autumn and the color white. Its body parts are the large intestine and lungs. The fifth element is water, representing emotion, flexibility, and wisdom. Water is connected to winter and the color black, and its body parts are the bladder and kidneys.

One of the Yellow Emperor's wives, Leizu, was also exceptionally innovative. One day, she was sitting in her garden, drinking tea in the shade of a mulberry tree. A sudden breeze caused the cocoon of a silkworm moth to fall out of the tree. Plop! It landed in Leizu's hot tea.

Leizu looked at the cocoon and noticed it was dissolving. Curious, she stuck her finger in the tea and pulled on the unraveling string. It was over three hundred feet long.

Empress Leizu told her husband about the silk thread from the cocoon. "It is lustrous and smooth! I wonder if I can weave it into cloth?"

Huangdi nodded and smiled. "By all means, investigate this matter!"

Leizu explored the mulberry trees in her garden, studying the silkworms' life cycle, learning how to raise them. She discovered that female silkworm moths laid hundreds of eggs on mulberry leaves, and when the larvae hatched, they immediately began feeding on the leaves. After growing and molting several times over three weeks, the silkworms raised their upper bodies off the leaves and started swaying. The empress learned this was the time to gather them onto frames, as each caterpillar would soon form a cocoon of silk thread.

Leizu's workers put the cocoons in boiling water and unraveled the silk. She also invented a reel for winding the thread, which would be dyed and woven into cloth on a silk loom, another of Leizu's inventions. The Chinese kept their silk-making process as a state secret, which gave them a monopoly on the silk textile trade for centuries.

Court ladies pound silk cloth to soften it. '

Chapter 2:
The Jade Emperor's Realm

Who was the Jade Emperor? He was the supreme deity in Taoist mythology. He headed a celestial hierarchy with a pantheon of gods and goddesses under him. The Jade Emperor was a pivotal figure who governed the heavens and the Earth. Was he the same as Shangdi? How did he rise to power and maintain order and justice among the gods? This chapter dives into these questions and also investigates other significant deities in his court.

China's Spring and Autumn period (772-476 BCE) was a tumultuous time in the Zhou dynasty when vassal kings took advantage of weak emperors. Despite messy politics, China's culture flourished under the "Hundred Schools of Thought," an era when several major philosophies emerged under the teachings of K'ung (Confucius), Laozi (Lao Tzu), and Mozi. Laozi developed Taoism (Daoism), possibly influenced by earlier teachings.

Taoism was a philosophy that later developed into a religion. Laozi taught that "Dao," or "the Way," governed the universe, bringing natural order. Dao (Tao) was not a deity but a fundamental principle, the underlying force that creates and sustains harmony and balance. Laozi never mentioned the Jade Emperor. He was more concerned with the philosophical side of things—most importantly, achieving oneness with Dao. He said that oneness with Dao occurred when a person remained uninvolved with the things of the world, lived a simple life, disregarded self-interest, and had no attachments to anything.

Laozi wrote the *Tao-Te-Ching* (*The Book of the Way*), a poetic guide about emptying oneself of pride and yielding to life's ups and downs. As time passed, Laozi's followers struggled with not worshiping anything. Yes, Dao was a divine principle, but one cannot offer sacrifices to a principle. To whom should they pray? Over the centuries, Taoism evolved into a religion with gods and goddesses. Emperor Xuanzong (712-756 CE) declared it the state religion of the Tang dynasty and mandated that everyone study Taoist scriptures. He elevated Laozi to the status of a royal ancestor and established a school for Taoist teachers.

This was when the Jade Emperor became the most important god in Taoism. Before the Tang dynasty, he was unknown or perhaps a deity in Chinese folk religion. Now, he

Ming dynasty silk painting of the Jade Emperor [5]

was Heaven's king. The Chinese referred to their supreme deity as "Yu Huang Shangdi" or "Jade Emperor, the highest god." In the Tang dynasty, the Jade Emperor was a manifestation of Shangdi. He ruled the cosmos and lived in the highest Heaven with his family and officials in a splendid palace.

One tradition regarding the Jade Emperor's origins said he was always a god. Another said he was a man who became a god. In the second version, he was a soldier and minor official named Zhang Denglai. He died in the 1046 BCE Battle of Muye that ended the Shang dynasty and began the Zhou dynasty. He and the other soldiers who died were at the "Terrace of Canonization" in the afterlife. A deceased nobleman named Jiang Ziya was passing out rewards—positions in Heaven's hierarchy—for those who were the most valiant in the battle. He filled all the positions but one, the Jade Emperor.

Jiang Ziya coveted the Jade Emperor's position, but it would be unseemly to appoint himself, so he waited for the other soldiers to offer it to him. When they did, he modestly replied, "Děng lái" ("Wait a second"). He did not want to appear too eager. However, in Chinese, "Denglai" was also the name of the brave soldier. (This is one example of puns in Chinese stories.) Zhang Denglai stepped forward to receive the reward, and Jiang Ziya could not lose face. He had no choice but to award Zhang Denglai the position of Jade Emperor.

Another Jade Emperor origin story took place in the Kingdom of Miraculous Joy and Heavenly Lights. The aged, infirm king had no sons, so his queen prayed for a son to be the crown prince. One night, she dreamed of the philosopher Laozi and miraculously conceived. (Inexplicable, conceptions were a common theme in Chinese folklore.) The baby was surprisingly advanced for his age. He walked and talked much earlier than ordinary babies.

The child impressed everyone with his calmness, gentleness, and concern for others. He helped the poor and disabled, and was respectful to everyone high and low, even the animals. When the king died, the prince became king. After stabilizing and enriching his kingdom, he journeyed to the Bright and Fragrant Cliff to meditate, study, and cultivate Dao. He achieved his aim and became immortal.

As an immortal, the king became an assistant to Yuanshi Tianzun, "Heaven's Lord of Primordial Beginnings" (probably Shangdi). One of his duties was to assist the people of Earth in fighting demons. The most powerful demon had recruited an army of malevolent spirits to conquer Heaven and rule the universe. The gods rallied to defend Heaven, but he overcame them.

The Jade Emperor saw an ominous glow in Heaven and flew upward to challenge the formidable demon. In a horrendous battle in which the mountains quaked and tidal waves swept the seas, the Jade Emperor defeated the daunting demon and scattered his hellish horde. In Chinese mythology, Heaven's rulers did not reign forever. Yuanshi Tianzun appointed the Jade Emperor to succeed him as the supreme god of Heaven, where he maintained order and justice among the gods.

Even today, Taoists and Buddhists worship the Jade Emperor on the ninth day of the Chinese New Year. They burn incense and offer vegetables, cakes, fruit, and wine on an altar decorated with paper lanterns. Worshippers kneel and prostrate themselves before his image in their homes or Taoist temples.

The Jade Emperor's wife was Wang Mu, and the couple had seven daughters. One of their daughters was Zhinu, the weaver goddess. Her job was to weave the colorful sunsets and the Silver River (Milky Way). Every day, with her magical robe, Zhinu flew down to Earth to bathe in a stream. A herdsman named Niu Lang saw her and was enchanted by her beauty. He snatched her magic robe, which she used to travel between Earth and Heaven.

"Bù kĕ néng! (No way!)" Zhinu screeched. "Give me back my robe! I can't get back to Heaven without it."

"What about Heaven on Earth?" the saucy shepherd asked. "Come to my house and be my bride!"

Zhinu cocked her head and looked at the handsome herdsman. She shrugged and went with him. When the Jade Emperor heard, he was livid. Yet, his daughter was with the shepherd of her own free will.

After some time, Zhinu found the chest where her husband had hidden the magic robe. She was lonely for her parents and her home in Heaven, so she used the robe to visit them. Once she arrived in Heaven, the Jade Emperor threw the Silver River (Milky Way) between Heaven and Earth. Zhinu had woven it, and now it blocked her way back to her shepherd.

However, the Jade Emperor was touched by his daughter's wails when she could not return to her husband. "Sweet daughter, you belong here, but once a year, you can visit your shepherd. I will make a bridge over the Silver River on the seventh day of the seventh moon each year."

The Lyra constellation is east of the Milky Way, and the star Vega represents Zhinu. The Aquila

Chang'e, the Moon Goddess ⁶

15

constellation is west of the Milky Way, and its Altair star represents Niu Lang. In early autumn, the Milky Way appears dimmer because its brightest part, the galactic core, is less visible. Thus, Zhinu can cross it.

Among the other significant deities in the Jade Emperor's court was the Moon Goddess, Chang'e. She was not always a goddess. Once, she was a stunningly beautiful woman with hair as black as night, skin as white as milk, and cherry-red lips. Her husband was the celebrated archer Hou Yi. At that time, the world had ten suns instead of one, making the Earth too hot for people to survive. Hou Yi shot down nine of the suns, leaving only one, which gave the correct amount of warmth and light.

Wang Mu, the Queen of Heaven, visited him in mid-autumn, rewarding him with the Elixir of Life. "If you drink half of this vial, you will live forever. If you drink it all, you will become a god," she told him.

Hou Yi could not decide what to do with the elixir. What good was it to live forever if his wife would die one day? What good was it to be a god if his wife was still a mortal? He gave the vial with the Elixir of Life to his wife, Chang'e, before going out hunting. "Keep this safe for me until I decide what to do with it," he said.

However, Hou Yi had a student named Peng Meng with a treacherous and conniving heart. He had been with Hou Yi when Wang Mu gave him the elixir. After Hou Yi left for the hunt, Peng Meng burst into his house. Chang'e was playing with her pet rabbit and screamed when she saw the intruder.

"Give me the Elixir of Life!" Peng Meng snarled.

Realizing the darkness of his heart, Chang'e knew she could not let him have it. If he became immortal, he would be a demon. To keep it from Peng Meng, she grabbed the vial and drank it all. Still holding her rabbit, she floated out the window and into the sky. Peng Meng ran off, never to be seen again. That night, Hou Yi came home, and his wife's maid told him what had happened.

Hou Yi ran outside. "Chang'e! Chang'e! Come back to me!" he cried.

He realized the moon was exceptionally bright, and then he saw the shape of the rabbit on the moon. "She's up there! She's the Moon Goddess now."

He called the servants and said, "Quick! Put an altar here in the courtyard and place little cakes and fruit on it! We must honor my wife, who has become a goddess."

From that time until today, the Chinese people gather to celebrate the Mid-Autumn Festival, eating "moon cakes" stuffed with delicacies.

Caishen, the God of Wealth (Zhao Gongming)⁷

Caishen, the god of wealth, was also at one time a human named Zhao Gongming. When the Qin dynasty (221-206 BCE) came to power, he retreated to Mount Zhongnan to cultivate Dao. Once he achieved Dao, he became immortal but did not become the god of money until the Tang dynasty (618-907 CE). Initially, the Jade Emperor made him the Lieutenant Marshal of the Divine Clouds, one of the Five Gods of Pestilence. (They did not send pestilence; they protected people from it.)

In this role, Caishen commanded the clouds to send thunder, lightning, wind, and rain. He oversaw law and order among the people, exacting punishment for the guilty but showing mercy to those who repented. He and his fellow gods healed sicknesses and protected people from epidemics, such as the plague. Once he became the god of money, he helped people build financial fortunes but also policed fair trade and honest business practices.

Some images of Caishen show him riding a tiger. He has a black face and beard and wears an iron crown. He might hold a whip, a sword, or a money bowl. At Spring Festival (Chinese New Year), Chinese people invoke Caishen's blessing as they greet each other with "Gōngxǐ fācái," which literally means, "Congratulations! May you get rich!" At Chinese New Year, married adults give red envelopes with money to children and young, unmarried people. Employers give bonuses in red envelopes to their employees.

A sword, snake, lute, and parasol are symbols of the Four Heavenly Kings who were immediately under the Jade Emperor in Taoist and Buddhist theology. The Four Heavenly Kings guarded the world's four cardinal directions (or, sometimes, the four corners). Artwork of the Four Kings usually shows them wearing full armor, and each holds one of the four objects.

Duowen Tianwang, the "King of News," guards the north. He hears everything and carries an umbrella because he brings rain. Zengchiang Tianwang, the "King of Growth," guards the south and carries a sword. He causes roots to grow and rules the wind. Chiguo Tianwang, the "Upholder of the Kingdom," guards the east. He carries a lute, which he plays to bring people to the "way," or the truth. He protects all the people and animals in the kingdom. Guangmu Tianwang, king of the west, sees everything. He carries a snake, which to the Chinese represents change, renewal, and transformation because the snake can shed its skin.

The Four Heavenly Kings ⁸

While defending Heaven and Earth, the Four Heavenly Kings and the Jade Emperor clashed with a cheeky supernatural creature called Sun Wukong, or the Monkey King. A Chinese poet and politician named Wu Cheng'en recorded his exploits in the novel ***Journey to the West*** in the Ming dynasty (1368-1644 CE). He based it on earlier

Chinese folktales and dramas. *Journey to the West* is a fanciful and fictional work, but it is based on the quest of a real monk named Xuanzang (602-664 CE). He traveled to India to study Buddhist scriptures and bring them back to China.[i]

Sun Wukong, the monkey, did not have an ordinary birth. At the top of Mount Huaguo, the "Mountain of Flowers and Fruit," lay a magic stone. When the world was young and the goddess Nuwa was mending the sky, she had dropped one of her colored stones on the mountain. It lay there for millennia, absorbing the rays of the sun and moon and receiving nourishment from yin (Earth) and yang (Heaven). One day, the rock broke open, and inside was a stone egg. As the wind blew on the egg, it hatched, and out popped Sun Wukong, a stone monkey.

At first, the monkey could only move his eyes. When he did, two golden beams shot toward Heaven, alarming the Jade Emperor. "What was that?" the Jade Emperor said, turning to two officers. "Go down to the mountain and find out what is going on! Where did that bright light come from?"

By the time the officers arrived at the mountain, the stone monkey was eating and drinking regular food, losing his stoniness and becoming more like a regular monkey. He had met some wild monkeys on the mountain and was playing with them in a stream. The officers reported to the Jade Emperor what they found. "He doesn't seem to be anything special," they said.

But on the mountain, Sun Wukong, the monkey, was curious about the stream. "Where does this water come from?" he asked.

The other monkeys shrugged. "Somewhere up on the mountain."

"Let's find its source!" Sun Wukong said. He led the other monkeys, following the stream until they reached a waterfall.

"This must be the source of the spring!" the monkeys said. "Whoever goes under the waterfall to the other side will be our next king!"

Sun Wukong took the challenge and bravely plunged into the waterfall. When he did, he entered the "Water Curtain Cave." He called back to the monkeys on the other side of the waterfall: "Everyone, come in here! Look at this cave. It will be our secret palace!"

---

[i] Cheng'en Wu, *Monkey: Journey to the West*, trans. Arthur Waley (Penguin Classics, 1994).

The monkeys passed through the waterfall and joined him in the cave, pronouncing him their new king.

"I'm now 'Handsome Monkey King'!" Sun Wukong laughed.

However, his joy soon faded. His dear friend, an old monkey, died. This was the first time Sun Wukong saw death. "There must be a way to defeat death! I won't rest until I find out," he determined.

Monkey King made a raft and floated down the river, searching for an immortal sage to instruct him in the way of Tao.

A Chinese actor portrays the Monkey King.⁹

After wandering for weeks, the Monkey King finally found a Taoist temple where the sage Puti Zushi taught martial arts and meditation. Puti Zushi refused to teach the Monkey King, but Sun Wukong dug in his heels and sat at the gate to the temple, waiting. Months later, Puti Zushi asked one of his students, "Is that monkey still out there?"

"Yes, he is."

"Āiyā!" the sage exclaimed, smacking his forehead. "He's not going away. Alright, invite him in. I must say, that monkey has fortitude!"

So, the Monkey King joined the temple, where Puti Zushi taught him Taoist principles and martial arts. Sun Wukong learned to fight with a staff. Through discipline and meditation, he acquired special powers, such as shapeshifting into other animals or objects, and the Cloud Somersault, where a single leap would carry the monkey for miles. Puti Zushi also taught him the secret of immortality through the "seventy-two heavenly methods of transformation."

"Never practice these skills in front of other people just to show off," he warned the monkey. "If you do, other people will aspire to be your students, but they might use the skills for evil. And tell no one who taught you these things. Swear it!"

When the Jade Emperor discovered that the Monkey King had become immortal and learned formidable warrior skills, he gave him a minor position in Heaven's court: Keeper of Horses. "I want him up here, where I can keep an eye on him," the Jade Emperor explained.

Later, after the Monkey King found out that he had Heaven's lowest position, he abandoned Heaven and returned to his mountain cave. Sun Wukong discovered that when he was gone, the Demon King of Confusion had been kidnapping the monkeys from the mountain and enslaving them. The Monkey King killed the demon and rescued the monkeys. Then, he put up a flag advertising himself as "Heaven's Great Sage."

Chapter 3:
Legends From the Silk Road

The Silk Road was not one highway. It was a transportation network linking China to trade with India, Thailand, Indonesia, Central Asia, and eventually Africa, the Middle East, and Europe. The preferred route was by sea, not land. Fleets of ships sailed from the South China Sea into the Indian Ocean, then up the Persian Gulf or the Red Sea. Camel caravans on the Silk Road's land routes traversed China's western deserts and high mountains, extending into India, Afghanistan, and beyond.

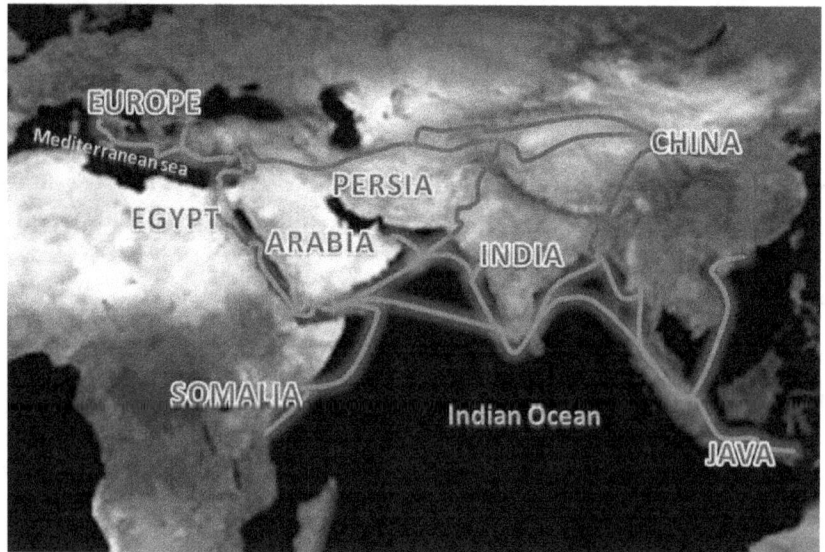

The Silk Road traveled over land and sea. [10]

China exported silk cloth and silk thread to Syria and Lebanon. The Syrians of Damascus used the thread to weave their renowned damask cloth, a luxury item named for their city. The Phoenicians of Tyre also wove silk and dyed it with the coveted purple dye made from murex sea snails. China exported Panax ginseng to Syria, and the Syrians shipped it to Italy. China imported horses and spices from Persia, glass from Egypt, and perfume and precious metals from India. Ships and caravans constantly plied the seas and deserts, transporting goods back and forth. Along with the commodities came new ideas, religions, and innovations. The Silk Road exchanged not only merchandise but also culture.

With such diverse cultural interchange, countless tales emerged of merchants and mythical creatures encountered along the ancient trade routes. Some were renowned historical figures, such as Zhang Qian. Others were legendary heroes who fought bandits and monsters on the intercontinental routes. Their stories symbolize the peril and promise of travel along these treacherous highways and sea routes.

Zhang Qian, known as the "Father of the Silk Road," was an explorer and diplomat during the Han dynasty. His 138 BCE expedition to the Fergana Valley opened the door for China's trade to the West. In his day, China had newfound strength after being led by several powerful emperors. However, the fierce, nomadic Xiongnu tribes made travel through the eastern Eurasian Steppe perilous.

Up to this point, China had small, stocky Mongolian ponies, but news came that "Tianma," or heavenly horses, were being bred in the Fergana Valley (today's southern Kyrgyzstan, eastern Uzbekistan, and northern Tajikistan). "These horses are tall and exceptionally strong!" the reports said. "They can run like the wind, carrying a fully armored man."

Emperor Wudi appointed Zhang Qian to lead an expedition over the Tian Shan Mountain Range (in today's Xinjiang Province). With ninety-nine men, Zhang Qian left the Chinese capital of Chang'an (today's Xi'an). He traveled around the far western end of the Great Wall of China and into the Taklamakan Desert. People gasped when they heard of his planned route. "No one has ever crossed that desert and lived to tell the tale," they murmured.

Sure enough, the Xiongnu captured Zhang Qian's group, enslaving them for over a decade. However, Zhang Qian married a Xiongnu woman, who helped him gain the trust of the Xiongnu chieftain. Finally, Zhang Qian escaped with his guide, his wife, and his son. They pressed on with the desert crossing, then climbed the Tian Shan range with its 24,000-foot mountains. Emperor Wudi's jaw dropped when Zhang Qian stumbled back into China's imperial court thirteen years after he left.

"I thought you were dead!"

"It's all true!" Zhang Qian told Wudi. "There really are heavenly horses! Unfortunately, the people of Fergana refuse to sell them to us."

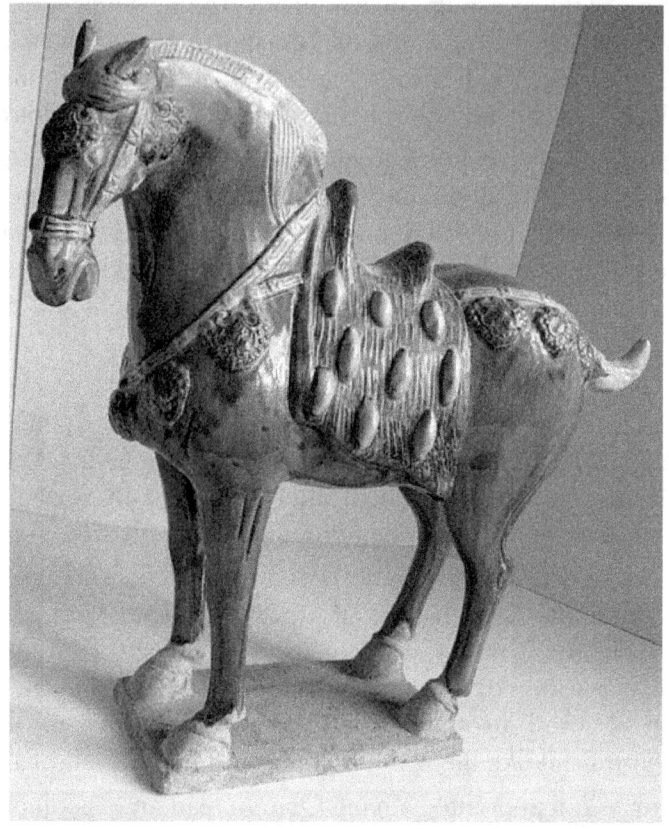

A ceramic Fergana warhorse buried in a Tang dynasty tomb [11]

Wudi frowned. "If the people of Fergana refuse to sell horses to us, we'll take them! And we'll deal with the Xiongnu on the way."

The emperor sent sixty thousand soldiers over the mountains and desert to Fergana, and they captured a herd of horses to bring back to China to breed. They also drove out the Xiongnu.

Once China controlled the Tarim Basin of today's Xinjiang, caravans began traveling from China to the west and northwest, carrying silk to trade for furs, gemstones, and ivory. It opened a whole new world to China. Eventually, the Chinese heard about Rome in the far-distant west.

China's silk enchanted the aristocratic Romans, who paid a fortune in gold for the luxurious fabric.

As merchants traveled along the Silk Road, they would stop to rest at desert oases or wayside inns. Travelers from all over paused for a few hours to water their camels or stay the night.

A favorite pastime in these resting places was storytelling. Carpets were a key trade item on the Silk Road, and travelers rested on these as stories were told. (Western China produced knotted wool carpets as early as 1000 BCE, particularly in Khotan on the western edge of the Taklamakan Desert.) Some stories on the Silk Road involved a flying carpet or a magic carpet, which, in Taoism, symbolized spiritual transcendence in the journey toward enlightenment. The Jewish and Arabian versions of the stories describe a rug that transported a man through the air.

China had its own charmed carpets. One Chinese folktale known as **The Enchanted Tapestry** is the story of a widow who spent many years weaving a magical rug that depicted a fantasy world. She pricked her fingers and used her blood for the deep red colors, weeping as she wove her masterpiece. Fairies frequently flew into her house to watch her weave the exquisite rug. When she finally finished weaving, the pictures in the tapestry seemed to come alive. The flowers swayed, and the animals danced.

When the fairies reported back to the gods of Sun Mountain in Tibet, they sent a magic wind to snatch up the rug and fly it to the mountain. The woman sent her three sons to retrieve it. To take back the tapestry, they had to complete a series of perilous and nearly impossible tasks. The two oldest sons thought it was too hard. Then, a sorceress approached them, bribing them with jewels to abandon their quest. They returned to their mother. "We couldn't get the rug, but look! We brought you these jewels!" they said.

Yet, their mother only wanted the tapestry that she had wept and bled over. Meanwhile, the youngest brother was working his way through the tasks set by the gods of the mountain. He had to climb the Mountain of Fire, then cross the Sea of Ice. Finally, he arrived at Sun Mountain to find fairy princesses weaving copies of his mother's rug. Weary from his long journey, he fell asleep and awakened the following morning to find the rug rolled up next to him. He took it home to his mother, who laughed with joy when he walked in with her beloved tapestry. As he crossed the threshold, the scene on the rug transformed into a real paradise where he and his mother lived from that point on.

A highly sought-after commodity on the Silk Road was rare gemstones. Naturally, tales told around the fire revolved around jewels. An ancient Chinese folktale was the "Marquis of Sui's Pearl." The ruler of the Sui state was inspecting his domain when he came across an enormous python in dire straits, dying from a hideous wound. The marquis stopped the bleeding and bandaged the wound. Grateful, the snake circled him three times, then slithered off.

A year later, the marquis was traveling through the same region on an inspection tour. One night, he dreamed the snake was sending him a giant pearl from its crown as a gesture of gratitude for saving its life. He awakened to find a lustrous pearl lying on the pillow next to him. The ruler treasured the precious pearl, which glowed with the brilliance of gratitude.

The Azure Dragon on the Ming dynasty (1889–1912 CE) national flag [18]

Travelers on the Silk Road frequently passed by cemeteries for those who succumbed to harsh conditions, disease, or brutal attacks by bandits. Among the graves, they noticed carvings of mythical creatures, including the Azure Dragon, the Black Tortoise, the Vermilion Bird, and the White Tiger. These creatures were manifestations of the Four Heavenly Kings, representing the four cardinal directions. The ancient Chinese believed these creatures protected the caravans.

The most famous mythical creature to travel the Silk Road was Sun Wukong, the Monkey King, who journeyed to India in search of Buddhahood. As you may remember from chapter two, ***Journey to the West*** describes his mythical adventures, based on the sixteen-year pilgrimage of Xuanzang, a real-life seventh-century monk. Folktales, poetry, and dramas of Xuanzang's journey had circulated for centuries. A central character in the story was Tang Sanzang, who represented Xuanzang. Tang Sanzang, the "Longevity Monk," was found in a river as a baby. He was a reincarnation of the Golden Cicada, a disciple of the Buddha.

The impudent Monkey King was back in Heaven at this point and had been stirring up chaos. The Jade Emperor was at his wits' end. He tried jailing Sun Wukong and even attempted to kill him, but the clever creature always escaped. Finally, the Jade Emperor asked the Buddha for help. The Buddha traveled from his temple in India to meet with the Jade Emperor in Heaven. Sun Wukong brazenly leaped between the Buddha and the Jade Emperor.

A painting of the monk Xuanzang on his way to India[18]

"I should be the next Jade Emperor!"

A collective gasp arose in Heaven at Sun Wukong's irreverence. The Buddha raised one eyebrow, then turned to the Jade Emperor. "I see what you mean. He's incorrigible."

He reached down and picked up the Monkey King, balancing him on his hand. "I bet you cannot get out of my palm."

The Monkey King laughed and rushed off. He ran to what he thought was the edge of the universe, where he saw five high pillars. "I've reached the end of existence!" Sun Wukong exclaimed. He hopped about, peeing on one pillar and writing graffiti on another: "Sun Wukong is the Great Sage equal to Heaven."

The Monkey King ran back to the Buddha, only to find that what he thought were pillars were the Buddha's fingers. He had never left the Buddha's palm. Yet, at that point, he suddenly did, as the Buddha threw him down to Earth, sending a mountain of rocks to cover him. Only his hands and head stuck out from the bottom of the mountain. Sun Wukong remained imprisoned for five hundred years.

"Stay there until you learn humility and patience!" the Buddha sternly admonished him.

After five centuries, the Monkey King heard that Guanyin was looking for pilgrims to travel west with a monk named Tang Sanzang. Guanyin was a bodhisattva, a person who had achieved enlightenment but delayed entering the transcendent state of nirvana to help others reach Buddhahood. (Guanyin was originally a man in India, but the Chinese later portrayed him as a woman.) She was now helping others on their path and was looking for pilgrims to travel to India with Tang Sanzang to bring Mahayana Buddhist scriptures back to China.

The Monkey King sent Guanyin a message: "I'll happily serve Tang Sanzang on his pilgrimage to Tianzhu (India) if you set me free from this mountain."

Guanyin had heard that the Monkey King was impossible to control. She gave Tang Sanzang a magic golden circlet. "Once the Monkey King puts it on his head, it will never come off. I'll give you a sutra to chant if he is naughty. The circlet will tighten, giving him a dreadful headache. It will remind him of the restraint required in Buddhism."

Guanyin then visited the Monkey King, giving him three

A Song dynasty (960–1279 CE) painting of Guanyin [14]

hairs. "If you are ever in an impossible situation, use one of these hairs," she instructed. "They will transform you into something that will enable you to escape."

The Monkey King set off on the pilgrimage to India with Tang Sanzang. He redeemed himself by faithfully focusing on the task at hand, which was to assist and protect Tang Sanzang. He put into play the martial arts skills that Puti Zushi had taught him centuries earlier. Part of the small group was Zhu Bajie (Pigsy), Sha Wujing (Sand Monk or Sandy), and Bai Long Ma (White Dragon Horse). They served alongside the Monkey King as bodyguards to atone for their past sins.

Pigsy had a pig head and a human body. He overate, and was lazy and easily distracted by pretty women. He once saw the Moon Goddess, Chang'e, and tried to seduce her. Heaven punished him by giving him a pig's head. Tang Sanzang regularly reminded him of the "eight restraints" of Buddhism: don't kill, steal, misbehave sexually, lie, get drunk, or eat after noon. Avoid luxury and mindless entertainment. Despite not being an exemplary Buddhist, Pigsy possessed some impressive powers. He could flip yin and yang (turning cold to hot, day to night), trigger earthquakes, and ride on clouds.

Sandy had once been a general in Heaven until he broke a jade goblet during the Heavenly Peach Festival. Was it an accident, or did he do it on purpose? The Jade Emperor assumed the latter, sentencing him to eight hundred swats with a rod. Then, he sent Sandy to Earth, where he reincarnated as a man-eating monster with a red beard and blue skin who lived in quicksand. He carried a magic rod and wore a necklace of skulls (victims he had eaten). Guanyin converted him to Buddhism, and he became a model disciple, loyal and obedient to Tang Sanzang, as well as kind-hearted and polite toward his fellow pilgrims.

Tang Sanzang rode on the White Dragon Horse, who was the son of the Dragon King of the West Sea. The Dragon King had accidentally burned a precious pearl given by the Jade Emperor and was sentenced to die. Guanyin pleaded for his life and then sent the dragon to the Yingchou Stream, which flowed from Shepan Mountain, to wait for Tang Sanzang.

However, when the monk arrived, the dragon failed to recognize him and ate his white horse in a single gulp. Then, he launched into battle with the Monkey King. Just then, a Tudigong, or earth deity, whispered to the Monkey King, "Guanyin sent the dragon! He's supposed to help Tang Sanzang."

Sun Wukong stopped fighting the dragon, who transformed into the White Dragon Horse that carried the monk on the journey.

Monkey King, White Dragon Horse, Tang Sanzang, Pigsy, and Sandy in a painting from Beijing's Summer Palace[15]

Sometime later, the Yellow Robe Demon, who lived in Moon Winds Cave, captured Tang Sanzang so he could eat him. The White Dragon Horse tried to save the monk but failed. "Pigsy!" he cried. "Go to Flower Fruit Mountain and get the Monkey King!"

Shortly before this happened, a Cadaver Demon named Lady White Bone tried to capture Tang Sanzang. She wanted to eat the monk, thinking it would make her immortal. The demon transformed into a beautiful princess to deceive Tang Sanzang. However, she did not fool the Monkey King. He smacked the "princess" with his staff. The demon shapeshifted into an old lady and then into an elderly man. Both times, the Monkey King saw through her disguise and finally killed the demon.

Sun Wukong's actions horrified the monk. He did not realize that the princess, the old lady, and the old man were all personifications of a demon. He thought the Monkey King was abusing and killing innocent people, so he banished him from the pilgrimage. Sun Wukong returned to Flower Fruit Mountain and his monkey subjects.

So, when Pigsy rushed to the mountain, begging him to come save Tang Sanzang, the Monkey King frowned. "The monk banished me!"

Pigsy appealed to his vanity. "I know, Monkey King, but he was mistaken. You must rescue him! You're the only one who can! By the way, you'll never believe what that Yellow Robe Demon said about you."

This triggered the Monkey King into action. He flew back to save Tang Sanzang; however, the Yellow Robe Demon blew him away with a fierce gust of wind. But the indomitable Monkey King flew back and continued fighting until he rescued Tang Sanzang from the demon's cave.

Tang Sanzang needed bodyguards because bandits were always a threat on the Silk Road. Demons and other supernatural creatures were constantly on the attack, thinking they could become immortal and super-powerful if they ate the monk. The pilgrims suffered eighty-one tribulations on the journey, but these perils were part of the testing they had to endure to achieve their spiritual goals. As they traveled, Tang Sanzang instructed them in Buddhist teachings and encouraged them to lead virtuous lives.

The Monkey King used several supernatural martial arts tactics when defending the pilgrims. One was the Cloud Somersault, a leap and flip that covered 34,000 miles. To activate this spell, he spoke an incantation, made a special hand sign, clenched his fist, and then shook his body. Sun Wukong also used the Seventy-two Transformations, which allowed him to shapeshift into a variety of animals or objects. It also enabled him to become invisible, change the weather, heal, or teleport.

After a harrowing journey, Tang Sanzang and his group reached India's (real) Vulture Peak, home of the (legendary) Thunderclap Monastery. The pilgrims acquired the sacred scrolls they were seeking and returned safely to China. For his faithful service and stellar defense of the pilgrims, the Monkey King became spiritually enlightened and attained Buddhahood, with the title "Victorious Fighting Buddha." His golden circlet, which tightened when he misbehaved, disappeared.

Chapter 4: Tales of the Lotus Pond

The prince and poet Cao Zhi, who lived in China's Three Kingdoms period (220-280 CE), once said, "Of all the plants in the world, the lotus flower is unique." In his poem "Ode to the Nymph of the Luo River," Cao Zhi compared the goddess to the flower: "She is as luminous as a lotus emerging from clear ripplets."[i]

Sacred lotus [16]

---

[i] Robert Joe Cutter, *The Poetry of Cao Zhi* (De Gruyter, 2021).

Ponds with floating lotus flowers are an integral part of China's landscape. Lotus flowers hold special significance in Chinese legends, as they symbolize purity, enlightenment, and rebirth in both Buddhist and Taoist traditions. The ancient Chinese perceived lotus ponds as transformed realms where divine creatures and enlightened beings lived.

In Chinese legend, **He Xiangu** was a breathtakingly beautiful yet chaste young woman who became one of the Ba Xian—the Eight Immortals of Taoism. As with most Chinese names, the first name "He" was her surname. Her given name, "Xiangu," means "fairy aunt." Artwork of Xiangu often depicts her with a lotus, as her story illustrates the transformational and purifying qualities attributed to the flower.

Who were the Eight Immortals? They were originally human beings who became "Xian," celestial or immortal beings. Together, they fought against evil and injustice. He Xiangu was the only woman, although one of the other immortals, Lan Caihe, was a man who wore women's clothing. The Eight Immortals lived on an island group in the Bohai Sea (the top part of the Yellow Sea off northeastern China's coast). No one else could approach the island because the "weak" water surrounding it could not support a ship's weight. Because they were avid wine drinkers (a common practice in northern China), their nickname was the "Eight Drunken Immortals." They reportedly introduced Zui Quan (Drunken Kung Fu), characterized by swaying, unpredictable, and stumbling moves.

When He Xiangu was born in the Tang dynasty, legend says that a purple mist surrounded the house. Six long hairs hung from the infant's head, a portent of greatness. By the age of four, she had incredible strength, enabling her to lift heavy things.

As a young teen, He Xiangu went up the mountain to pick tea with some other girls. She got distracted while searching for the right leaves, and when she looked up, she could not see her friends. The young girl was walking up the path, looking for her companions, when she saw an ancient man with a long beard, a six-tiered robe, and a tall cap. As she drew closer, she realized he had blue eyes, something she had never seen before. He was Lu Dongbin, a scholar and poet who had lived for 250 years in his human body and was now one of the Immortals.

Lu Dongbin was probably the first teacher of neidan shu (inner alchemy), which focused on extending one's physical life and enabling one's spirit to live eternally. Neidan employed Taoist meditations and other practices to understand the connections between the spiritual, natural, and bodily realms. Lu Dongbin would eventually invite He Xiangu to become one of the Eight Immortals, but first, she needed to prepare herself.

The Eight Immortals crossing the sea. He Xiangu stands at the stern, holding the rudder. Her collar represents the white lotus."

He told her to eat powdered mica (a colored or transparent sparkling mineral that separates into thin leaves), explaining, "If you do this, you will become delicate and light, and on the path to immortality."

He Xiangu followed Lu Dongbin's instructions, which also included being sexually celibate and eating very little food. When she looked at the glistening mica, Xiangu saw celestial flowers—white lotus buds (probably hallucinating due to starvation). She became so thin that many people thought she was a wraith (ghost) even when she was still a mortal.

Following custom, He Xiangu's parents arranged a marriage for her. Yet, on the night of the wedding, she disappeared. She left a note behind, explaining that marriage was an earthly distraction from the destiny the gods had ordained for her. Instead, she said, "I shall listen to the phoenix playing the flute in the moonlight while riding the celestial crane on the journey to immortality."

He Xiangu riding the celestial crane in a sixteenth-century Taoist painting[18]

After receiving instructions in a dream, He Xiangu began eating mother-of-pearl as part of the path to immortality. This enabled her to transcend her physical body and glide effortlessly through the air, over the hills. She gathered herbs on her flying excursions, which she brought home and studied to learn how to use them to heal people. She is associated with the white lotus because it is a symbol of health, harmony, and well-being.

One day during the reign of the Tang dynasty Emperor Zhongzong, He Xiangu flew up to Heaven and became one of the Eight Immortals. Artwork of Xiangu often portrays her as a young, ethereal woman with delicate features and long black hair, holding a lotus flower in her hand.

The **Dragon King's Daughter** is the story of how a little girl called Longnu (Dragon Girl) became the first female Buddha.

In the Buddhist religion, there is not just one Buddha. Buddhism arrived in China via the Silk Road from India in the first century CE during the Han dynasty. The first Buddha was Siddhartha Gautama, who founded Buddhism in India. The word "Buddha" means "awakened," referring to those who have achieved enlightenment by truly understanding reality and detaching from impermanent things. When they achieve Buddhahood, suffering is extinguished, and they enter the state of nirvana, or perfect freedom. In Buddhism, the lotus flower is a symbol of the transcendence of worldly desires.

The little girl's story is told in the *Lotus Sutra*, the primary scripture for Chinese and other East Asia Buddhists. Longnu's father was Sagara, the Dragon King. He was a naga, half-human and half-serpent. Sagara lived in a palace at the bottom of the ocean and ruled over the rain.

At the tender age of eight, Longnu was renowned for her intelligence, keen memory, and understanding of the lives of people and animals. She memorized lengthy Buddhist mantras using "dharanis," or mnemonics and chants. Longnu could enter deep meditation and understand the dharmas—the Buddha's teachings on how elements of the empirical world connected.

Eager for enlightenment, Longnu reached a state of non-retrogression. This is a stage a Buddhist disciple reaches when they are certain they will continue to progress spiritually into higher levels of existence without backsliding or giving up. It is the point of no return on their journey to Buddhahood. In this stage, Longnu's compassion extended to all people and animals as if they were her children. She was harmonious and merciful to all.

Manjushri was a bodhisattva who embodied transcendent wisdom. The *Lotus Sutra* records that Manjushri was proud of Longnu's progress and spoke about her

A silver figure of Manjushri holding a lotus [19]

approvingly when he was asked if anyone could attain Buddhahood quickly:

> "The daughter of the Dragon King has just turned eight. She has deep wisdom and a keen perception of people's activities and motivations. This little girl has mastered the dharanis and understands a storehouse of the Buddha's profound secrets. She has entered into deep meditation and has attained no regression. The blessed child can understand and teach competently and comprehensively."

At that moment, Longnu, the Dragon King's daughter, arrived at Vulture Peak, where the Buddha was. Sariputra, one of the Buddha's chief disciples, scoffed when he saw the little girl:

> "Do you think that in such a short time you have attained the Way? I find this hard to believe! You're a girl! A woman's body is defiled, incapable of receiving the Law. And that's not all! The journey to Buddhahood is extensive. It takes immeasurable time for a person to receive formal instruction and practice good deeds. As a female, five obstacles stand in your way! A woman cannot become a Brahma. She cannot become a Sakra, lord of celestial beings. A woman cannot become a devil king or a sage king. She cannot become a Buddha. So how can you attain Buddhahood so quickly?"

Longnu did not answer Sariputra. She was holding a precious jewel in her hands, worth more than all the treasures on earth. The Dragon King's daughter walked up to the Buddha and gave him the jewel, which he instantly accepted.

Longnu turned to the others. "Did you see him accept my gift without hesitation?"

"Yes! Immediately!" Everyone nodded.

Longnu smiled. "Now, watch me achieve Buddhahood. It will happen even faster!"

Within a second, the Dragon King's daughter transformed into a man. In the blink of an eye, in Longnu's new male form, he performed all the duties of a bodhisattva. He then traveled to the Spotless World of the South (the Pure Land), where he sat on a jeweled lotus and attained enlightenment. He explained and expounded on Buddhist law to people and creatures everywhere. Women, dragons, and animals were all ecstatic that it was indeed possible for them to achieve enlightenment.

Statue of Longnu in Thailand's Hatyai Buddhist Theme Park.[20]

Besides her story in the *Lotus Sutra*, Longnu appeared in Chinese folklore, recorded in the *Precious Scroll of Sudhana and Longnu*. In this narrative, Longnu is an acolyte of Guanyin, the Bodhisattva of Compassion, alongside Shancai (Sudhana), also known as "Red Boy." Shancai first appeared in *Journey to the West*, where he was a monster that shot inextinguishable fire from his mouth. He got into a fierce battle with the Monkey King when he tried to eat Tang Sanzang, the monk. The Monkey King asked Longnu's father, the Dragon King, to send rain, but it did not put out Red Boy's fire. Shancai transformed himself into a lookalike of Guanyin to deceive the Monkey King.

When the Monkey King realized the deception, he went to the real Guanyin for help. Hearing the Red Boy had pretended to be her, she was furious. Guanyin extinguished the fire and gave Monkey King a confusion spell to use against Red Boy. After battling the Monkey King and Guanyin, Red Boy finally surrendered and became Guanyin's student.

At this time, the very young Longnu had not yet begun her journey to Buddhahood. Yet, as the daughter of the Dragon King, she had special powers. One day, Red Boy was walking through the mountains when he heard a little girl crying. He looked down and saw a bottle containing a tiny snake.

"Please! Get me out of this bottle!" the snake said.

Red Boy uncorked the bottle and set her free, but then the snake, Longnu, transformed into a dragon.

"Don't eat me!" Red Boy screamed in terror.

"I'm a dragon. We eat people. It's the way of the world," she replied.

"But I just rescued you from the bottle!" Red Boy cried.

"Oh, alright!" Longnu sighed. "Let's have three judges hear your case and decide whether your good deed outweighs nature."

The first judge, the Water Buffalo Star, sided with Longnu. He had been kicked out of Heaven and badly treated by humans, so he had no sympathy for them. The second judge, a Taoist priest, also sided with the dragon. He avoided involvement in earthly matters, believing events should follow their natural course.

The third judge was a little girl who likewise took Longnu's side: "Yes, you can eat Red Boy. You can even eat me! But first, show me how you could fit into that little bottle."

Longnu shapeshifted back into a little snake and slithered into the bottle. The girl instantly plugged the bottle, entrapping Longnu. Then the girl transformed into her true identity, Guanyin.

"Please, I beg you for mercy!" Longnu cried.

"If you want to be saved," Guanyin told her, "you must study enlightenment at the Grotto of the Sounds of the Flood."

And that is how Longnu became a student of Guanyin and began her path to Buddhahood. Ironically, Longnu had to transform into a man to achieve enlightenment. However, Guanyin had been a man in India but shifted into a woman when she came to China after becoming a bodhisattva. (It's possible that the Chinese misinterpreted Indian paintings and sculptures of Guanyin. Men often appeared somewhat androgynous in Indian religious art.)

The Butterfly Lovers, or **Liang Shanbo and Zhu Yingtai**, is among several Chinese folktales that feature the lotus or lotus pond as a motif for spiritual union and eternal love. The lotus pond at Liangzhu Cultural Park in Ningbo, Zhejiang Province, China, commemorates the lovers. Along with the lotus pond, the park also features terraces, pavilions, the Nine Dragon Pool, sculptures of the lovers, and an ornamental bridge symbolizing marriage.

Here's how the story goes.

Zhu Yingtai was the pretty and intelligent daughter of a wealthy father. One day, as a young teen, she marched up to her father and said, "I want to go to school!"

"Yingtai, my darling, only boys go to school. You've already learned how to read and write here at home."

"I know, Baba, but it isn't the same! The boys are studying the Chinese masters, learning philosophy and the classics. I want to do the same!"

"My sweet daughter, they won't let a girl into the school."

"I'll disguise myself as a boy. And my maid will come with me, also in disguise."

After her father relented, Yingtai and her maid headed to the boarding school, dressed as boys. While traveling, Yingtai met a handsome boy named Liang Shanbo, who was on his way to the same school. They quickly became friends, and Shanbo considered Yingtai his brother. However, Yingtai soon fell in love with Shanbo.

After three years, Yingtai's father sent a message telling her to return home, as he had arranged a marriage for her. However, Yingtai was deeply in love with Shanbo, who still did not know she was a girl. Shambo accompanied Yingtai on the first eighteen miles of her journey home, but despite several hints, he did not guess Yingtai's true gender.

Before the wedding, however, Shanbo traveled to Yingtai's village to visit her. He was shocked to discover that his "brother" was a girl! He now realized that he was in love with her, and they vowed to be together forever.

Shanbo approached Yingtai's father, asking for her hand in marriage.

"I have already betrothed her to another," the father explained. "My family will lose face if we break the agreement."

Shanbo stumbled off, weeping. He could not bear to face life without his beloved Yingtai. He refused to eat and withered away. "I'm going to die soon," he told his servant. "Bury me by the side of the road where Yingtai will pass by on her wedding day."

Finally, the fortune teller picked out an auspicious day for the marriage. The women clothed Yingtai in a scarlet dress and draped her with jewels. Her friends and family escorted her toward her fiancé's village with much fanfare—music, firecrackers, and red banners proclaiming good fortune over the marriage. Suddenly, a wild windstorm tore down the road, forcing the wedding party to take shelter. Yingtai looked out from her decorated sedan chair, realizing they had stopped by Shanbo's grave.

The bride stepped down from her palanquin and approached her lover's burial place. Suddenly, a clap of thunder rang out, and the grave opened. Without hesitation, Yingtai threw herself into the gaping hole. At that moment, the storm stopped, and the sun came out. Yingtai's family approached the grave but could not see her. Then, to their astonishment, two butterflies fluttered out of the opening in the ground, spiraling upward until they disappeared into the sky.

The Butterfly Lover's sculpture at Liangzhu Culture Park[21]

Chapter 5: The Gift of the Dragon

Even today, the dragon holds a pivotal role in Chinese culture. While Westerners typically consider dragons to be fire-breathing, malevolent creatures, the Chinese believe dragons are complex. They can sometimes create chaos, but they can also be benevolent, bringing favorable fortune and strength. The Chinese dragon is associated with water and weather, making it a revered figure in agricultural societies for its rain-making ability, which brings prosperity. In ancient times, the dragon was closely associated with the emperor. Today, it embodies the Chinese spirit.

Every year, the Chinese celebrate the **Dragon Boat Festival** (Duanwu Jie) in May or June. They eat sticky rice dumplings, race dragon boats, and pray for good luck. The Chinese believe that the fifth day of the fifth month (Double Fifth Day) is especially unlucky. On this day, people are likely to be stung by scorpions, bitten by snakes, or stricken with sickness. Dragon Boat races counteract evil.

Dragon boats are long, narrow, uncovered boats propelled by a team of paddlers. The boats have a dragon head at the bow and a dragon tail curling up from the stern. Brightly painted reptilian scales cover the hull.

Three Chinese stories, loosely based on historical events, connect to the Dragon Boat Festival. One is the story of **Qu Yuan**, a highly respected poet and government official in the Warring States period (475-221 BCE). He was part of the Chu royal family and served as an advisor to King Huai. However, he had rivals in court. When facing an invasion by King Zhao of Qin, Qu Yuan proposed a strategic alliance with other Chinese states. His enemies at court slandered him, insinuating that he had ulterior motives for allying with other states. King Huai believed them and exiled Qu Yuan. Failure to heed Qu Yuan's warnings brought disaster. King Zhao of Qin captured King Huai, and he died in captivity.

Qu Yuan mourned his king and, in his poetry, lamented the Chu state's decline. He grew frail and ultimately committed suicide by throwing himself into the Miluo River. When the local people saw him fall into the river, they jumped into their boats and rowed to rescue him. After realizing they were too late, they threw sticky rice dumplings wrapped in bamboo leaves into the water as an offering to the river spirits. (Qu Yuan wrote about offering sacrifices to the water spirits in his lifetime.)

A Qing dynasty cloisonne enamel depiction of the Dragon Boat Festival [22]

Another Dragon Boat story connects to the tale of **Xi Shi**, one of the "Four Great Beauties" in ancient China. Xi Shi lived in eastern China during the late Spring and Autumn period. Legend says that when she leaned over a lotus pond, the carp stopped swimming in awe of her stunning beauty. The entire idiom is, "Beauty that makes the fish sink, and flying geese fall to the ground. The moon blushes, and flowers close their blooms."

King Goujian of the state of Yue gifted Xi Shi as a concubine to King Fuchai of Wu. Goujian had suffered a defeat at the hands of Fuchai in battle and was forced to pay tribute. The "gift" was a "sexpionage" operation. Xi Shi and another lovely lady were actually secret agents. The two charming young women so enchanted King Fuchai that he neglected affairs of state to spend all his time with them, especially Xi Shi.

King Fuchai built the "Palace of Beautiful Women" in a rural setting and spent more time there than in his capital. He took Xi Shi riding around in his carriage and followed her advice. When she told him she disliked his chief military advisor, the king handed a sword to General Wu Zixu, ordering his loyal military commander to kill himself. Then, he ordered his servants to throw Wu's body into the river.

With General Wu gone and King Fuchai ignoring the safety of his realm, King Goujian swept in with his army, utterly overwhelming Fuchai's forces. In remorse, Fuchai committed suicide. The people of eastern China began worshiping General Wu as the "God of the Waves." They considered him responsible for the Qiantang River's tidal bore (a surge during high tide), the largest in the world. Eventually, the Dragon Boat Festival in eastern China became associated with General Wu.

A third tale connected to the Dragon Boat Festival was about a girl named **Cao E** who lived in eastern China several hundred years after General Wu. When Cao E was thirteen, her father fell into the river while paddling a dragon boat in the races. The people searched for seventeen days but could not find his body. Finally, Cao E waded into the river and disappeared.

Five days later, her body resurfaced, holding her father's body. The local people considered this an astounding example of filial piety—respect and love for one's parents and ancestors. They immediately began worshiping her and built a temple in Cao E's honor. Today, in Shaoxing, Zhejiang Province, the local people hold a memorial service at her temple during the Dragon Boat Festival.

A silk Kesi tapestry of a dragon [28]

The tale of **Yu and the Dragon Gate** takes us back to when Gonggong, the water god, banged his head on one of the four pillars that held up the sky and unleashed the Great Flood. This version of China's flood story happened at the beginning of the Xia dynasty (2070–1600 BCE), China's first dynasty, before the development of writing. In this version, the flood was localized in the Yellow River Valley, the cradle of Chinese civilization. The floodwaters continued for years, destroying the cities and farms along the Yellow and Yangtze rivers.

Historians once thought the Great Chinese Flood and even the Xia dynasty were mythical. However, recent archaeological evidence suggests a significant, prolonged flood occurred in the Yellow River Valley near the beginning of the Xia dynasty.[i] An earthquake caused a landslide, which dammed the Yellow River where it flows from the Tibetan Plateau and through the Jishi Gorge. Because of this discovery, some historians moved the beginning date of the Xia dynasty to 1900 BCE. This is also when the Yellow River Basin transitioned from a Neolithic culture to a Bronze Age civilization.

The Han dynasty historian Sima Qian recorded the myth, saying the Yellow and Yangtze rivers and their tributaries all flooded for two generations.

> "King Yao moaned, 'Like endless boiling water, the flood is pouring forth destruction. Boundless and overwhelming, it overtops hills and mountains. Rising and ever rising, it threatens the very heavens. How the people must be groaning and suffering!'"[ii]

King Yao sought advice from the "Four Mountains" (perhaps four major gods or the four pillars that held up the sky). They told him to make his distant cousin Gun his flood control manager. Yet, Yao's sorcerer sniffed, "This will not end well!"

King Yao had no other option, so he appointed Gun to deal with the flooding. Gun put the people to work building dams to control the flood. Yet the surging water was so strong that it broke the dams. After nine years of failure, Gun stole some divine soil called "Xirang" from Heaven. When he built dams with this material, it expanded when touched by water, successfully controlling the flooding. Everyone breathed a sigh of relief.

---

[i] Qinglong Wu, et al., "Outburst Flood at 1920 BCE Supports Historicity of China's Great Flood and the Xia Dynasty," *Science* 353, no. 6299 (2016): 579-582,
https://www.science.org/doi/10.1126/science.aaf0842

[ii] Qian, Sima. "Shiji, Records of the Grand Scribe," *China Knowledge: An Encyclopaedia on Chinese History and Literature*, accessed March 13, 2025,
http://www.chinaknowledge.de/Literature/Historiography/shiji.html

However, the god of Heaven found out that Gun had stolen his dirt. "Kill him!" he ordered Zhurong, the god of fire. "Get my dirt back!"

So, Zhurong killed Gun, retrieved the Xirang, and brought it back to Heaven. Immediately, disaster struck the Yellow River Basin again. The dams collapsed, and the floodwaters submerged the land. The people laid Gun to rest in a tomb, but his body did not decompose. Three years later, Yu emerged from his belly as a dragon. By this time, King Yao had resigned in disgrace. The new ruler, King Shun, ordered Yu to finish the work his father had started. Instead of building dams, Yu opted to create channels to drain the water into the East China Sea. He used a channel-digging dragon and a mud-hauling turtle to assist his engineering efforts.

Jishi Mountain stood in the way, so he tunneled through it. Then, he encountered another mountain, which he split in two, calling the gap "Longmen" or "Dragon Gate." As the river flowed through the Dragon Gate, it created a spectacular waterfall. Yu continued to build his channels to drain the water from the Yellow River Basin, splitting or tunneling through more mountains. After thirteen years, Yu successfully drained the excess river water into the East China Sea. With the floodwaters gone, the people rejoiced, and King Shun made Yu his successor. Yu "the Great" began the Xia dynasty and ruled for forty-five years.

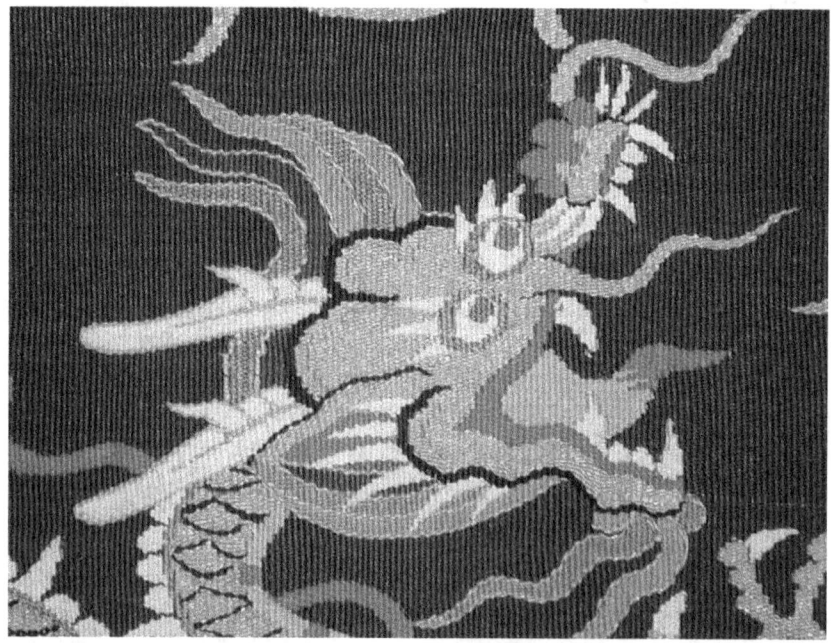

A silk and metallic thread dragon tapestry on a Ming dynasty imperial court robe [14]

Dragons guarded Yu's **Longmen (Dragon Gate)**. Carp would try to jump up the steep waterfall. If they could make it through the Dragon Gate without being eaten by dragons or eagles, they would transform into a dragon. The pounding water, jagged rocks, birds of prey, and dragons stopped most fish. Yet, some carp pressed on, determined to reach the top and become dragons.

A playful little carp lived in a lake near the bottom of the Dragon Gate. One day, his grandfather called him over:

"Xiao Yu, do you see that stream flowing into our lake? It passes over multiple waterfalls before reaching here. If you swim up that stream and jump up the waterfalls, you will reach the highest waterfall. It is nearly impossible for a fish to climb. Yet, if you conquer your fear, survive being caught by foxes or birds, and jump to the top of the falls, you will transform into a dragon!"

"A dragon!" the little carp breathed. "I'm going to try!"

Xiao Yu swam up the stream, jumping over the waterfalls, until he reached the bottom of the Dragon Gate. All he could see was mist at the top of the cleft from which water cascaded down. Many other fish were trying to leap up the waterfall, but the swift current pushed them down, or birds of prey caught them. Xiao Yu leaped from ledge to ledge up the falls, staying close to the falling water where the eagles and hawks could not catch him.

Finally, he reached the top, where a dragon guarded the gate. "Don't even think about getting through the gate," the dragon laughed. "You're just a little fish, not worthy of becoming a dragon."

Xiao Yu smiled. "I might be a little fish, but are you really a dragon? You can't even fly!"

"What do you mean? I most certainly can fly!" the dragon huffed.

"Show me!" Xiao Yu challenged.

The angry dragon spread its wings and flew up into the sky, leaving the gate unguarded. Xiao Yu flicked his tail and passed through the gate. Suddenly, he started transforming into a dragon. The dragon guard flew back and said, "Well, I see you tricked me! Yet, I'm happy for you. You showed ingenuity and bravery! You deserve to be a dragon."

Even today, the Chinese idiom "Lǐyú lóngmén" or "Carp jumps the Dragon Gate" means to take a sudden leap forward in circumstances. Specifically, it was used for students who passed the imperial civil service examinations, providing an opportunity for boys from lower- or middle-class families to become government employees.

The guardian dragon (top) and Xiao Yu (bottom) as a new little dragon [25]

Our last dragon story is the **Monkey King and the Dragon King**. This tale takes place before Sun Wukong, the Monkey King, went on the pilgrimage to India. He had briefly served in Heaven until he found out he had the lowest job. So, he returned to Earth and his monkeys, just in time to rescue them from the Demon King of Confusion. To ensure his monkeys would not be enslaved again, Sun Wukong stole weapons from a nearby country to arm his band. Yet, he could not find a suitable weapon to arm himself. Then, Sun Wukong heard that Ao Guang, the Dragon King of the East Sea, had a magnificent collection of weapons.

Ao Guang was a chaos-causing dragon, bringing hurricanes and droughts and disregarding the Jade Emperor. The people offered lavish sacrifices to keep the dragon from wreaking havoc. One day, a seven-year-old divine creature named Nezha took a bath in Jiuwan Stream. His movements sent shockwaves through the underwater aquifer, and the tremors even disturbed Ao Guang in his palace beneath the sea.

Irritated, the Dragon King sent Li Gen, a nature spirit, to find out what was happening, but Nezha killed him. When the Dragon King received this news, his son, Ao Bing, volunteered to avenge Li Gen's death. However, Nezha killed Ao Bing too.

"Enough is enough!" the Dragon King snarled. "I'm going to go see that youngster's father!"

Nezha's father was Li Jing, the Pagoda-bearing Heavenly King. His pagoda could capture any demon or god, and he was a canny military strategist who enabled China to defeat its enemies. When the Dragon King arrived at Li Jing's court, Nezha confessed to his crime. "Yes, I killed your son. I pulled out his tendons to make a belt for my father. Here they are. You can have them."

The Dragon King held his son's tendons in his hand, smoldering. "Li Jing! You must sacrifice yourself to atone for your son's sin!" he demanded. Yet, Li Jing refused.

The Dragon King stormed out, exclaiming, "I'm filing a complaint with the Jade Emperor!" He flew up to Heaven, now embarrassed that he had never offered sacrifices to the Jade Emperor. Nezha also flew up, arriving at Heaven's gates at the same time as the Dragon King. Nezha ambushed and thrashed him, ripping his scales from his body. He forced the Dragon King to shapeshift into a small snake and carried him back to Earth.

The Dragon King struggles with Nezha. [36]

Ao Guang transformed back into a dragon, vowing to round up the other dragon kings and wreak vengeance. When the four dragon kings captured Nezha's parents, Nezha panicked. "Leave them alone!" he pleaded. "I'll give you my internal organs if you release them!"

The Dragon King agreed to the exchange and flew back to Heaven with the intestines as an offering to the Jade Emperor. Sometime later, Sun Wukong, the Monkey King, arrived at the Dragon King's undersea palace, in need of a special weapon. The Dragon King told his guards to send him away, but Sun Wukong pushed his way in.

"Sir!" he said to the Dragon King, "I'm a king, just like you! I would like you to give me a weapon."

The Dragon King furrowed his brow. "Now I know who you are! You studied under Puti Zushi! I have heard that you have exceptional powers. You even served in Heaven as the Jade Emperor's Keeper of Horses."

"Yes," the Monkey King nodded modestly. "But now I'm living on Earth again. I need to protect my monkeys from the demons. Can you help me?"

The Dragon King ordered his servants to bring out an array of weapons. Yet, none was powerful enough for Sun Wukong. Then, the Dragon King's wife spoke up. "What about the Ruyi Jingu Bang?"

The Ruyi Jingu Bang was an iron rod with gold rings on each end that magically expanded or shrank. Yu the Great had used it to measure the water during his flood management campaign.

The Dragon King seemed puzzled by his wife's suggestion. "It's a tool, not a weapon!"

"Yes, but it's been glowing recently," she explained. "I believe it's trying to communicate something to us."

When the Monkey King came close to the rod, the Ruyi Jingu Bang glowed brightly. When he reached out to touch it, it shrank down so he could hold it like a staff.

The Dragon King nodded. "This is the weapon meant for you!"

When he heard about this, the Jade Emperor erupted in rage. "What was the Dragon King thinking, giving Sun Wukong the Ruyi Jingu Bang? We will have no end of trouble!"

The Jade Emperor sent his warriors to capture the Monkey King. However, with the supernatural skills taught him by Puti Zushi and his magical Ruyi Jingu Bang staff, the Monkey King fought off all the celestial soldiers.

"Baozha ba! (Blast it!)" the Jade Emperor swore. "All right!" he said in exasperation. "Politely invite him back up here. Make him the guardian of the Celestial Peach Orchard. We need to keep a close eye on that troublemaker."

Heaven's peach trees only produced fruit every few thousand years, but eating the fruit gave supernatural powers. Sun Wukong helped himself to whatever peaches were ripe. After some time, Wang Mu, the Jade Emperor's wife, was planning her celestial peach banquet and sent her fairies to collect peaches for her guests. When the fairies discovered the Monkey King had eaten most of the peaches, they sucked air through their teeth in annoyance. "You stupid monkey! What is our lady going to serve her guests? You are definitely *not* invited to the banquet!"

"What?" laughed the Monkey King. "I thought I was the guest of honor! After all, I am Heaven's Great Sage!"

The fairies giggled. "To whom do you teach your wisdom? Everyone knows you're just the peach tree gardener!"

Deeply hurt, Sun Wukong sneaked into the banquet hall and stole some wine, then wandered around Heaven, creating mayhem until the Buddha finally imprisoned him under a mountain for five hundred years.

Chapter 6:
Bamboo and Its Significance

Bamboo is so deeply embedded in China's culture that another name for the country is Zhúzi Wángguó, or the Bamboo Kingdom. The largest member of the grass family, bamboo symbolizes virtue, resilience, integrity, and longevity. Bamboo can be a metaphor for a *jūnzǐ*, or a person of noble character, modesty, and flexibility. Because the wind bends bamboo but does not break it, the Chinese consider bamboo an example of standing firm when faced with fierce adversity.

While bamboo features prominently in Chinese artwork, architecture, mythology, and folklore, the Chinese appreciate its practical uses. Before inventing paper, the Chinese wrote on bamboo slips. Even today, they build rafts, cottages, and scaffolding from bamboo canes and weave baskets and chair seats from them. In the heat of summer, the Chinese enjoy sleeping on bamboo mats placed on their beds. The mats circulate air, keeping one cool.

The Chinese brew bamboo leaves for tea and wrap them around sticky rice for steamed dumplings. Young, tender bamboo shoots are a favorite food for people and animals. China's national animal, the giant panda, eats mostly bamboo—up to eighty pounds a day. Chinese musical instruments made from bamboo include the *dizi,* or side-blown flute, and the *xiao*, or end-blown flute. China's earliest firecrackers were hollow bamboo cane stuffed with gunpowder.

Several Chinese idioms center on bamboo. "Xiōng yǒu hang zhú" means "You must picture bamboo in your heart before you can paint it." The saying conveys the idea that one must carefully think out a plan before acting. "Pò zhú zhī shì" translates to "enough force to smash bamboo," meaning irresistible power. "Zhú lán dǎ shuǐ" translates to "drawing water with a bamboo basket," meaning wasted effort, because bamboo baskets leak like sieves.

Yuan dynasty (1271-1368) ink painting"

The story of the **Humble Farmer and the Magical Bamboo Stalk** highlights not only how bamboo brings wealth and good luck but also teaches the values of gratitude, humility, and perseverance. In ancient times, at the base of the emerald hills, sat a village, the home of a diligent farmer named Wei. He grew rice and wheat, toiling hard every day. Despite his efforts, Wei struggled to feed his family and provide for their needs.

His neighbors whispered, "That Wei! Our farms are all doing well, but he never seems to accomplish much."

Farmer Wei felt discouraged that his family was still deep in poverty. He had to contend with the whims of nature, like droughts, hailstorms, and savage windstorms that destroyed his crops. Finally, in the depths of despair, Wei wandered into the forest, ready to end it all. However, he encountered a hermit.

"Why are you here in the woods?" the hermit asked.

"I'm a failure!" Wei answered. "I am diligently working on my farm, but I cannot succeed. Can you give me a reason not to end my life?"

The hermit pointed to two plants. "What are these?"

"This one is a fern, and that one is bamboo," Wei answered.

The hermit nodded. "Which plant grows quickly?"

"The fern grows faster. Bamboo takes a long time to grow."

"That's right," answered the hermit. "Both the fern and the bamboo grow next to each other here in the forest and get the same amount of sun, nutrients, and rain. Yet, the young fern grows faster. However, later the bamboo catches up and grows ten times as tall as the fern. Do you know why?"

"Well, no," Wei answered. "I've never thought about it."

"Go back to your farm and your family," the hermit told him. "The answer will come soon."

Wei returned home and resumed farming. One day, in a neglected area of his property, he found an intriguing bamboo shoot that seemed to glisten with light. He carefully dug it up and transplanted it near his house. He meticulously fertilized and watered the glowing bamboo, but it did not seem to grow. Wei felt a kinship with the bamboo shoot. Months passed, and then years, but the bamboo was still a sapling.

His neighbors berated him. "Wei, why are you wasting so much energy on that little bamboo? It will never amount to anything. Stop your foolish dreams!"

Wei's wife consoled him. "Just ignore them, Wei. You're doing your best." Secretly, however, she worried about their finances.

Wei continued caring for his glistening bamboo shoot with unwavering faith. "Everyone thinks I'm mad, yet I believe I'm investing in this plant's hidden potential," he said.

In the fifth year, Wei emerged from his house one morning, stretching and yawning. He glanced at his bamboo shoot. "Wa!" he exclaimed. "Little bamboo! You are much taller this morning than you were yesterday!"

In the following weeks, his bamboo grew at an incredible speed. It rose another foot every hour. Within six weeks, it grew eighty feet high.

The villagers gathered around, their mouths gaping in shock. "Zhēn de ma? (Could it really be?) What kind of magic is this?"

Wei hurried into the forest, looking for the hermit. When he found him, he told him the story, and the hermit smiled and nodded.

"Was it magic?" Wei asked.

"Perhaps a little magic," the hermit said with a twinkle in his eye. "But it is also the payment for your years of continued faith, hard work, and patience. Not everything comes to us quickly. Sometimes, we must invest time and energy for many seasons before we see the fruit of our labor. All those years that you were watering and tending your bamboo shoot, its roots were growing under the ground. You couldn't see them, but they were laying the foundation for a glorious plant. The bamboo needed that root system to support the huge plant it would become."

Qing dynasty (1644–1912) ink and color on a silk painting of birds, bamboo, and camellias [38]

The **Devoted Dog's Bamboo Grave** is a tale of two brothers, Zhang Lan and Zhang Qin. When their parents died, Zhang Lan claimed entitlement to the house and most of the family's farmland, as he was the oldest. He also took the ox and chickens. Zhang Qin got only a small hut to live in, a tiny section of the farm, and the family dog.

Qin sat on a stool in front of his shack, scratching his dog on the head. "It's just you and me, Gǒu. Yet, I'm sure we'll succeed with teamwork and hard labor."

Lan was uninterested in strenuous work. He drank all the rice wine left in the house, then started eating the chickens. After eating all the hens, he had no source of eggs. He forgot to feed and water the ox enough to keep it strong. When he tried to plow the fields with it, the ox balked and refused to pull. Lan beat the animal mercilessly, but the ox kicked him.

"You stupid beast! Now you're my supper!" Lan yelled. He killed the ox and ate it.

When he sobered up the next morning, Lan realized he had no way to plow his fields and no chickens to lay eggs. What would he eat now? He walked over to his brother's hut.

"How are things going for you, Qin?"

"Well, it's not been easy," Qin said. "However, I taught the dog how to pull a plow! We don't have much land, but we've been working hard and growing vegetables. We have enough to eat and even a little to sell at the market so we can buy meat now and then."

"Wa! You taught the dog how to pull the plow? That's brilliant! Let me borrow Gǒu for a few days. My ox died, and I need him to plow my land."

Qin hesitated, knowing his brother was unkind to animals. Yet, he knew Lan needed to eat. "Okay, you can have him for a few days. But you must give him plenty to eat and drink and treat him well."

Lan took the dog to his land and put the plow harness on him. But Gǒu stiffened and refused to cooperate.

"Pull the plow, you stupid dog!" Lan yelled.

Lan kicked and beat the dog, but Gǒu would not pull the plow. Finally, Lan killed the dog and dropped its dead body in front of Qin's shack.

Weeping, Qin stroked Gǒu's head. He could not bear the thought of losing his companion. Qin buried his beloved dog in the corner of his garden.

Weeks later, Qin was surprised to see bamboo shoots springing out of the ground from the dog's grave. They quickly grew into a grove, giving shade for Qin to rest in after laboring on his small plot of land. One day during midday nap time, Qin was dozing under the bamboo. Plink! Something hit him on the head. He sat up, rubbing his head.

"Shénme? (What?)"

Plink! Plunk! Two more things hit his head. He looked down and saw three gold coins. Where did they come from? Qin leaped out of the way as a shower of coins fell from the bamboo. Gold coins covered the dog's grave.

"Oh, Gǒu! You good dog! Did you send these to me? Xièxiè! (Thank you!)"

Qin picked up the coins and poured them into a bag. He had enough money to buy a large farm and build a grand house. When Lan heard of his brother's good fortune, he came by to visit.

"Do you see that bamboo, Lan? It grew from Gǒu's grave. Gold coins are still falling from the bamboo!" Qin said.

Lan pretended to be happy about Qin's new wealth but secretly planned to steal the bamboo. "I'll plant it on my land and reap the gold!"

Lan ripped some of the bamboo from the ground, but as he did, dog excrement sprayed over him. "Āiyā!" he cursed. In a fit of anger, Lan broke the canes he had pulled up and stalked off.

Qin woke up the next morning to find the broken bamboo. He wept and raged yet gathered up the broken canes. "I'll weave a basket with these."

To his surprise, Qin discovered that coins filled the basket each night. Lan heard about the magical bamboo basket and asked to borrow it. "I need some money for my farm! It is your fraternal duty to help me."

Qin gave the basket to Lan, who hurried home with it. However, when he peeked into the basket the next morning, instead of coins, hissing snakes writhed inside it. He ran out of the house screaming and never bothered Qin again.

Bamboo and Turtle is a story about a twelve-year-old boy named Zhúzǐ (Bamboo), whose father was the keeper of the Sacred Tombs at Nanjing. Royal family members and other dignitaries were buried there. Bamboo watched with excitement one day as men carried ten sedan chairs with red velvet cushions. In them rode a group of the royal family visiting the tomb. Bamboo wanted to follow the procession as the imperial family moved through the area.

Qing dynasty painting of a dog and bamboo [39]

"Bamboo! Come back now! They'll think you're a beggar if you tag after them," his father sternly admonished him.

"Yes, Baba." Bamboo stood quietly in front of his house as the grand procession passed by.

Then, something caught his eye. The group had visited a small temple near his house, and the iron gate stood open. Many times, Bamboo had stood at the iron gate peering in at the temple. He could see into the temple's dark room. A pillar covered with inscriptions rested on the back of a giant stone turtle.

He was curious about the turtle and had asked his father, "Baba, why do they have a turtle in that temple? Why not some other animal, like a tiger?"

"It's just the custom," his father answered.

Now, Bamboo looked over his shoulder. His father had gone inside the house. Bamboo dashed over to the temple and hurried through the gate, into the courtyard, and through the temple door. He tripped and fell on its threshold and lay there, catching his breath, noticing the layer of dust on the floor. Then, he heard a noise, so he crawled under the stone turtle to hide.

"Careful!" rumbled a voice above him. "You're stirring up the dust! I'll be choking soon!"

It was the turtle's voice!

"I didn't know you were alive," Bamboo said in a quivering voice.

"There, there. Don't tremble so. But stop kicking up the dust!"

"I meant no harm," said Bamboo. "I've always wanted to see you."

"You wanted to see me?" Turtle chuckled. "Most people just want to read the inscriptions on the pillar resting on my back. The writing is all about emperors from the past. Yet, they barely look at me, and my father was one of the Four Benevolent Animals who assisted Pangu at the beginning of the world."

Bamboo gasped. "Your father was the Black Warrior of the North?"

"Well, my grandfather."

Bamboo's eyes opened wide in wonder.

"Quick!" Turtle commanded. "Run and close that gate, then come back. If your father notices it is open, he'll lock the gate. I want to tell you something when you get back."

Bamboo hurried out to the courtyard and swung the heavy gate closed. When he came back into the temple, Turtle remarked, "I'm weary of holding up this pillar for so many years. Yes, I know it is an honorable task, but my back hurts. Now that the gate is unlocked, I can escape."

"Oh, no!" Bamboo worried. "If you leave, the authorities will blame my father for leaving the gate unlocked. They'll cut off his head!"

"Don't worry! After I get outside the gate, sneak into your house and get your father's keys. Lock the gate, then put the keys back in place," Turtle instructed. "No one will know what happened. I'm too heavy for anyone to carry. They'll think it was the gods at work. This little temple will become famous!"

Bamboo began to weep.

"Why are you crying?" asked Turtle.

"I don't want you to go!" cried Bamboo.

"Then, come with me! We'll explore the world together!"

Bamboo looked at the heavy pillar resting on Turtle's back. "How will you get that off? It's too high to fit through the door."

"I've thought that through," said Turtle. "When I walk through the door, the pillar will hit the lintel, then slide off my back and onto the floor."

However, the escape did not go as planned. Instead of sliding neatly off Turtle's back, the pillar fell backward and smashed into pieces. Bamboo held his breath, terrified that his father would hear the commotion. Several minutes passed, and nothing happened. His father must be on the other side of the tombs, seeing the royal family off.

Turtle lumbered out of the gate, and Bamboo rushed home, grabbed the keys, and hurried back. He locked the gate, put the keys back in the house, and caught up with Turtle. Bamboo trembled with excitement. He had never been on an adventure.

"Where are we going?" he asked Turtle.

"To the place where my grandfather, the Black Warrior of the North, and the other benevolent creatures helped Pangu form the world."

"How far away is it?" Bamboo asked. "You can't walk very fast."

"Oh, we're not walking. We're flying!" Turtle laughed. "Hop on my back. We're traveling to the beginning of the world!"

Once Bamboo climbed up on Turtle's back, they rose in the air and flew faster than Bamboo thought possible. He looked down to see forests, villages, cities, and high mountains. Finally, Turtle flew to the ground. "Here we are! My friends will be here soon—Dragon and Phoenix. They were with my grandfather at the beginning of the world."

Just then, Bamboo heard flapping wings. It was a gigantic dragon!

"Ha ha, Dragon! I got here first. And you thought you could fly faster!"

Minutes later, the Phoenix bird flew in. Bamboo looked on in wonder as the creatures laughed, feasted, and shared stories. As night drew near, Turtle looked at Bamboo.

"It's time for me to go. I need to get Bamboo home before his father thinks he is lost," Turtle said.

Dragon gave Bamboo one of his scales as a memento, which turned to gold when it touched Bamboo's hand. Phoenix gave one of his fiery red feathers. Bamboo climbed onto Turtle's back, and they flew off through the clouds.

Yet suddenly, Bamboo felt himself slipping from Turtle's back. He screamed, realizing he was falling through the air. He saw a stand of tall bamboo below him and grabbed at the leaves to break his fall.

The next thing he knew, he felt his father shaking him, calling his name.

"Bamboo! Come out from under that turtle! How did you even get in here?"

Bamboo looked around. He was back in the temple, under the stone turtle. "Didn't I die?"

His father cocked his head. "You're very much alive, it's time for dinner, and you are covered with dust. Hurry home and clean yourself up! I need to lock this temple."

Turtle holding pillar at Prince Xiao Xiu's grave, 518 BCE[80]

Chapter 7: Phoenix Legends

Mythology in both the East and West featured the phoenix, called Fènghuáng in China. The Chinese believed that this mythical bird was involved with Heaven's primordial forces at the time of creation. It represented fidelity, justice, grace, and kindness. In the Western version, the phoenix passes through cycles of dying, only to be reborn from its own ashes. However, the Chinese perceived Fènghuáng as immortal, first appearing at the creation of the world. A Fènghuáng appeared when civilization was harmonious and prosperous but vanished in times of dissension and violence.

Even in the Neolithic era, the phoenix was a key element of Chinese culture. A shell mound in Hunan Province on the Yuan River, known as the Gaomiao archaeological site, dates to approximately 5000 BCE and features pottery with a phoenix motif. The ancient people of the Gaomiao culture were hunters, fishers, and rice farmers who were the first to develop white pottery on which they painted images, including Fènghuáng. The phoenix ceramics were unearthed in an area with an altar and a sacrifice pit, showing Fènghuáng had spiritual significance.

Artwork with the phoenix and dragon together first appeared in the Yangshao culture (5000-3000 BCE) in Shaanxi Province near Xi'an. The dragon and phoenix motif became highly popular in ancient China, with the dragon symbolizing the emperor and the phoenix the empress. They represented the harmony of husband and wife and also brought good luck. The phoenix was the feminine counterpart of the masculine dragon, representing the balance of yin and yang.

Twins were (and still are) considered a special blessing in Chinese families. A set of twins comprising a boy and a girl was especially auspicious, a sign of favor and fortune for the family. Even today, the Chinese refer to these boy and girl pairs as dragon-phoenix twins.

The phoenix's appearance in royal artifacts and architecture used by empresses highlighted its association with virtue and grace. In the Han dynasty, which began in 202 BCE, artists depicted a pair of phoenixes, male and female, on vases and other artwork. The male bird was "Fèng," and the female was "Huáng."

Fènghuáng, painted by Yu Sheng (1692-1767) [81]

According to Chinese mythology, after Pangu hatched from the cosmic egg at creation, Fènghuáng joined with the Dragon, Qilin, and Turtle to shape the cosmos. They created the five seasons (spring, summer, late Summer, autumn, and winter) and the five elements (earth, fire, metal, water, and wood). The phoenix ruled summer and fire, perceived as the giver of warmth and light.

The Four Benevolent Animals divided the world into five sections: east, west, north, south, and center. Fènghuáng, representing the south, controlled the five tones of traditional Chinese music, which are based on the pentatonic scale (gong, shang, jue, zhi, and yu). The phoenix sang to bring harmony to the heavens and held sovereignty over all the other birds. Fènghuáng symbolized the universe and the connection between Heaven and Earth. The bird's head was the sky, its eyes the sun, its back the moon, its feet the earth, and its tail the planets.

Fènghuáng was the herald of new dynasties. The Chinese believed that when the bird appeared, it was an omen of a new emperor coming to power who was not from the current ruling family. An emperor could lose the "Mandate of Heaven," the concept that Heaven gave the legitimacy to rule. The mandate depended more on the emperor's character than on his lineage. Only a virtuous, wise, and just ruler had Heaven's mandate.

The phoenix could not tolerate immorality. When evil reigned and vice took over, the phoenix disappeared. Fènghuáng refused to tolerate rulers who abused power or were deceitful. Such people would never see a phoenix. Floods and famines were signs that the current emperor had lost Heaven's mandate. If this happened, the Chinese could legitimately overthrow their emperor and install a new one. If people saw a Fènghuáng, it was a sign of blessing over the new dynasty.

A Fènghuáng would appear during the reign of benevolent rulers, confirming their legitimacy. When society lived in peace and harmony, the Fènghuáng was active in blessing the kingdom. When people saw the phoenix, it was a welcome sign that prosperity was coming their way. If they took note of where a Fènghuáng landed, a precious treasure was nearby. The Chinese phoenix was sheer goodness. It never sought revenge when wronged. It only blessed people, never cursing them. To avoid harming animals or even

Fènghuáng and Dragon on China's State Emblem from 1913 to 1928 [88]

plants, the bird subsisted on morning dew.

The Phoenix, the Dragon, and the Iridescent Pearl is a folktale about an adventure the pair had. Dragon enjoyed swimming in the cool river every day. Phoenix would accompany him but perch on a tree branch overlooking the river, as she did not want her feathers to get wet. One spring day, Dragon was enjoying a sunbath after his swim.

"Fènghuáng, if we followed this river downstream, where would it take us?"

Phoenix had traveled extensively, acquiring wisdom and knowledge. "Lóng (Dragon), my dear, it flows to the sea, as most rivers do," she replied.

"I have never seen the sea," Lóng remarked. "Fènghuáng, let's go on an adventure! We'll fly to the sea."

So Fènghuáng and Lóng flew into the air and traveled all day. They finally reached the seashore just in time to watch a glorious sky painted in pink, purple, and red as the sun sank under the waves.

"How beautiful! What an exciting day!" Lóng exclaimed. "Fènghuáng, I want to see more. Tomorrow, let's fly over the sea!"

The next day, the couple flew across the sea until they arrived at an island with palm trees and gleaming white sand.

"Wa!" Lóng exclaimed. "Such pure beauty! Look at these waterfalls and those lovely flowers. I have never seen anything like this!"

Fènghuáng agreed. "This truly is an exquisite place!"

The pair rested by a lake where the waterfall emptied. "Lóng! Look at that pebble on the lake bottom. It appears to be glowing."

Lóng peered down. "Maybe it's just the sun reflecting off it. Still, I'll dive in and grab it."

Minutes later, Lóng was back. "Look, Fènghuáng! It really is shining."

"Ah," Fènghuáng breathed. "This must be a precious stone!"

Below them, they heard a surly voice rising from the water. "Yes! It is quite precious. You are holding a magic pearl."

The two looked down to see a crab waving its enormous claws. "You must put it back immediately! The pearl's magic is why this island is extraordinary!"

"In that case, Fènghuáng, I think we must become the guardians of this pearl. We must preserve this enchanted island," Lóng said.

And so, the couple settled down on the lovely island. However, trouble was brewing in a distant land.

Luxuries surrounded a spoiled and self-indulgent princess, yet she always wanted more. She heard of the resplendent pearl on the magnificent island.

"I must have it for myself. Bǎobiāo!" she called her personal guard. "Go to that island and steal that pearl!"

The guard sneaked onto the island and stole the pearl when Lóng and Fènghuáng were enjoying their noontime nap. He traveled back to the distant realm and presented the priceless pearl to the princess.

"Ah! This must be the world's most glorious jewel. Look how it glows! My brilliant treasure, now you're mine!" she said.

But then, the princess frowned. "This glowing pearl is so bright, it's lighting up the sky. People will discover the cause of the radiance and find out that I stole it. We have to hide it away. Bǎobiāo! Take me to the mountain fortress!"

The princess hid the pearl away in an underground vault in the fortress. Yet, a few months later, she threw a birthday party for herself at the fortress. She could not resist bringing out the pearl to show her guests. The dazzling pearl was so bright that it was difficult to look at it directly. It glowed even more than when the princess first stole it, so brilliantly that it lit up the sky like the sun. It caught the attention of Lóng and Fènghuáng, who had been flying from one place to another, looking for the radiant pearl.

Fènghuáng flew at the speed of light toward the mountain fortress, swept through a window, and snatched up the pearl from the princess's hand with her claws. Flapping her wings, Fènghuáng flew out the window, but she had trouble holding on to the pearl. Suddenly, it slipped from her claw and dropped to the mountain. Fènghuáng dived after the pearl as it rolled down the slope. Suddenly, she heard a crash of thunder and saw a blinding light.

For a moment, Fènghuáng could see nothing. Then, she caught sight of the glowing pearl.

"Āiyā!" she exclaimed. "The pearl is melting!"

Just at that moment, Lóng caught up with her. "Look, Fènghuáng! The pearl is dissolving into water! See that spectacular emerald-green lake covering everything?"

Then, Lóng frowned. "Fènghuáng, I failed to protect the pearl when it was on the island. Now, it is my duty to guard the lake. I will never leave it! I will stand over it forever!"

In an instant, Lóng turned himself into a majestic mountain rising from the lakeshore.

"I will never leave you, my love!" said Fènghuáng. "I also must atone for letting the pearl be stolen." She transformed into a mountain guarding the lake's opposite shore. The emerald lake still glistens in China, with two high mountains standing guard on its shores.

Hui and the Golden Pheasant is a folktale about a peasant and a pheasant. The peasant, Hui, swindled a well-meaning man, but in the end, the man who was swindled was rewarded.

Hui was a farmer who struggled to make ends meet, yet he had grandiose dreams. He had raised a magnificent golden pheasant and decided to sell it in the city. He knew he would get a reasonable price for such a beautiful bird.

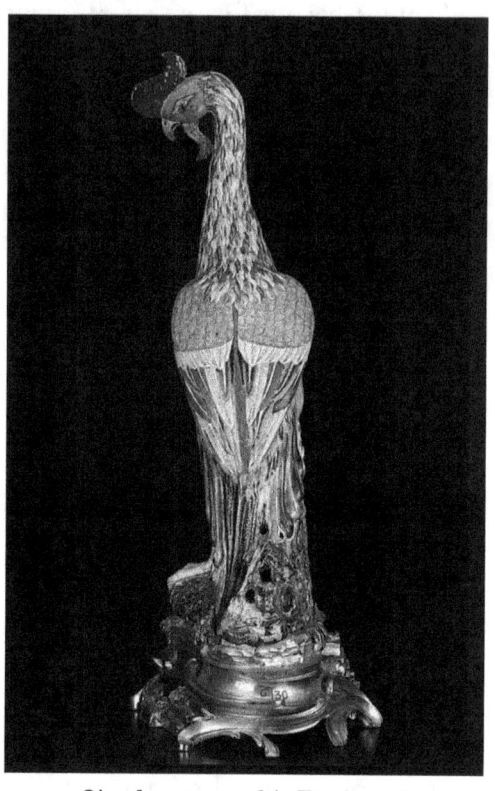

Qing dynasty porcelain Fènghuáng[88]

As he walked down the road carrying his pheasant in a cage, Hui daydreamed of what he would do with the money from selling the pheasant. "Maybe I could start my own business. Yes! I'll get rich and build a marvelous mansion. Then, a beautiful lady of means will fall in love with me, and we will get married. That's not all! I'll invent something ingenious. It will change people's lives and make me famous. I'll travel the world."

Hui's thoughts turned to Fènghuáng. "The bird always appears as a herald of favorable fortune and blessing. You, my lovely pheasant, are my Fènghuáng! You will bring me a wonderful future!"

Hui's fanciful fantasies were cut short when someone cleared their throat. It was a man named Enlai who had a curious nature.

"Excuse me," Enlai said. "I couldn't help but notice your broad smile. What is making you so happy?"

"Oh! My Fènghuáng is making me happy!"

"Your Fènghuáng?" Enlai questioned, puzzled. He stared at the bird in the cage. Wasn't it a golden pheasant? It had a bright golden head and back, a scarlet breast, and purple and blue on its wings and tail. He cocked his head in bewilderment. "Is this bird a Fènghuáng?"

"Oh, yes!" Hui smiled broadly. "This is my Fènghuáng. He will bring me immeasurable wealth and good fortune."

Enlai thought to himself, "If I buy this bird, I could give it as a gift to the king of Chu. He will consider it a sign of the Mandate of Heaven! Then, he will give me a substantial reward. I'll be rich and powerful!"

"May I buy your bird?" asked Enlai.

"Yes, but only at a high price."

Enlai was wealthy and considered the purchase an investment. "How about a thousand silver pieces?"

Hui cocked his head. "Make it two thousand, and it is yours!"

Enlai happily agreed and handed over two thousand silver coins. Hui handed him the cage with the pheasant.

Enlai excitedly traveled toward the capital of Chu, eager to take his expensive and invaluable gift to the king. It was a journey of several days, and he told everyone he met about the mythical bird he carried, which was to be a gift for the king. Word traveled fast, and soon the king heard about the gift coming his way.

Unfortunately, Enlai had forgotten to ask Hui how to care for the bird. He knew nothing about giving the bird water or what it liked to eat. After two days on the road, he spent the night at an inn and was horrified to find the bird dead the next morning.

"Oh! This is terrible! I did not know a Fènghuáng could die! Aren't they supposed to be immortal? Now, I have no gift for the king. I certainly will never see a Fènghuáng again!"

Several days later, Enlai received a message that the king wanted him to come to his palace. Enlai was confused, but he went anyway.

"Sir," he said to the king when he arrived. "I had hoped to bring you a fantastic gift. Sadly, now I cannot."

"I know," answered the king. "Word reached me that you were bringing me a Fènghuáng."

"I was, but he died."

"Yes, I heard. I did not know a Fènghuáng could die."

"Nor did I," sighed Enlai.

"Nevertheless, I am deeply touched by your intentions. Your thoughtfulness and largesse are beyond compare. Just knowing that you would bring me such an astounding gift is a blessing. For that, I will reward you!"

The king gave Enlai a position in his court and forty thousand silver pieces, twenty times what Enlai had paid Hui. The so-called Fènghuáng turned out to be auspicious for both Hui and Enlai.

Chapter 8: Warriors of Destiny

This chapter highlights the epic tales of legendary Chinese warriors with fates inextricably linked to the destinies of empires and realms. These heroes were famous for their unparalleled military expertise, exceptional bravery, brilliant strategies, and astounding combat skills.

These warriors had a destiny. In Chinese culture, the concept of destiny often signifies a preordained path that heroes are meant to fulfill, marked by trials and exceptional deeds. Destiny (mìngyùn) includes one's absolute, predetermined fate (mìng) plus elements based on one's choices, cosmic forces, and luck (yùn). Destiny is not entirely fixed; it has some flexibility. A person's actions and choices influence their lives.

Guan Yu

One of China's best-known warriors of destiny was Guan Yu (160-220 CE), a general at the end of the Han dynasty. Guan Yu possessed stellar military prowess, wielding a weapon called the "Green Dragon Crescent Blade." His weapon was a "guandao," a heavy, notched blade on a pole about five feet long. Guan Yu's history appears in the *Records of the Three Kingdoms*, written in the Sui dynasty (581-618 CE). By this point, people worshiped Guan Yu as a god. He was a dominant character in Luo Guanzhong's novel, *Romance of the Three Kingdoms,* written in the Yuan dynasty (1279-1368 CE).

When Guan Yu was in his early twenties, the Yellow Turban Rebellion, a peasant revolt, broke out. Near Guan Yu's hometown, a man named Liu Bei was reading a notice of the rebellion posted on a wall. He was a descendant of the fourth emperor of the Han dynasty, but his family had fallen into poverty after his father's death. Liu Bei was weaving straw sandals and grass mats to support his family. He sighed at the news of the revolt.

"Sir!" spoke a raspy voice behind him. "Why don't you help your country?"

Liu Bei swirled around to see a dark-skinned man with unruly hair. "Who are you?"

"My name is Zhang Fei. I have a farm near here, and I sell wine and meat."

Liu Bei introduced himself. "I'm a member of the imperial family, but we have fallen on hard times. I would love to fight for my country, but I have no money for armor or weapons."

"Well, I have the means to outfit a militia," Zhang Fei replied. "Why don't you and I raise some troops and defend our land?"

The two young men set off to the village inn to discuss their plans. Shortly after, Guan Yu walked into the inn and ordered wine. He was close to seven feet tall, with an eighteen-inch beard, a dark red face, and eyebrows that looked like silkworms.

"Bring it quickly!" ordered Guan Yu. "I'm on my way to join the army."

Liu Bei looked over his massive frame, then picked up his drink and sat down next to Guan Yu. "I'm Liu Bei. What is your name?"

"My name is Guan Yu. I used to live on the other side of the river, but I've been on the run for five years."

"Why?" asked Liu Bei.

"When I was a teenager, I killed a man. He deserved it. He was a thug and a bully who was hurting people. But he was also rich and powerful, so I had to leave town."

Liu Bei smiled. "My friend and I are putting together a militia to defend our country. Would you like to join us?"

Guan Yu nodded eagerly, and the three men walked off together to Zhang Fei's farm. "Let's go to the peach orchard behind my house," Zhang Fei said. "The flowers are in bloom. We should offer a sacrifice, asking for Heaven's blessing and swearing our intentions to fight together."

The *Romance of the Three Kingdoms* tells the story of the "Peach Garden Oath." Liu Bei held a ceremony in the peach orchard, where they sacrificed a white horse, a black ox, and wine. Liu Bei named Guan Yu as his younger brother and Zhang Fei as his youngest brother. The three men kneeled together and swore this oath:

> "Though we have different names, we are brothers. We swear to cooperate with each other, rescue each other, assist each other in times of distress and danger, honor our nation, and protect the people. May Heaven permit the three of us to die on the same day. May the gods confirm what is in our hearts, yet if we betray the brotherhood, or turn away from kindness and righteousness, may Heaven strike us down."

Guan Yu and Zhang Fei stood up and bowed before Liu Bei, offering him fraternal piety as their older brother. They then invited the local villagers to a feast, where they ate the ox and horse. Three hundred men came, and they recruited them for their militia. Some wealthy merchants helped outfit the new militia with horses, weapons, and armor. The three "brothers" fought together and were fiercely loyal to each other in the long struggle to reunite China. They slept in the same room and ate from the same pot.

However, they failed to preserve the Han dynasty. The uprising and other factors led to the Han dynasty's fall. A fragmented China entered the Three Kingdoms period (220-280 CE), during which warlords ruled three states. Liu Bei became the warlord over the state of Shu Han (primarily today's Guizhou, Sichuan, and Yunnan provinces in southwest China). He considered his state the legitimate continuation of the Han dynasty. Guan Yu and Zhang Fei became his generals and bodyguards.

Guan Yu was revered not only for his martial prowess, immortalized in folklore, but also for his loyalty, sense of honor, and strict code of behavior. His loyalty to Liu Bei was put to the test when Cao Cao, warlord of the Cao Wei kingdom in north China, captured him. Cao Cao and Liu Bei were archrivals, but Cao Cao had heard of Guan Yu's incomparable fighting skills. Instead of executing Guan Yu, he gave him gifts and offered him a position as an officer in his military.

Having no real choice, Guan Yu took the pragmatic route and served his new lord for a time. However, after killing Cao Cao's two arch enemies, Guan Yu politely refused Cao Cao's gifts.

"Sir, the best gift you can give me is my freedom," he said. "Let me return to my brother, Liu Bei. We have made an oath to fight together and die together."

Cao Cao released Guan Yu, who hurried back just in time to rescue Liu Bei from desperate straits. Years later, Guan Yu repaid Cao Cao for giving him his freedom. Cao Cao was fleeing a battle that had turned into a disaster for him. Instead of chasing him down, Guan Yu let Cao Cao escape.

Sun Quan was the warlord of the Wu kingdom in eastern China. While Lu Bei and Cao Cao fought each other fiercely, Sun Quan mostly stayed out of the fray. At one point, he allied with Lu Bei to successfully fight Cao Cao. Lu Bei and Sun Quan formed an uneasy alliance, and Sun Quan defeated Cao Cao.

However, Sun Quan criticized Guan Yu for stealing his food supply and constantly stirring up hostilities. His army succeeded in capturing Guan Yu. Sun Quan originally planned to keep Guan Yu alive to fight with him against Lu Bei.

But his advisors warned him against this plan. "A wolf shouldn't be kept as a pet as it'll bring harm to the keeper," they said. "Guan Yu and Lu Bei are sworn brothers. He will never agree to fight Lu Bei."

Thus, Sun Quan executed Guan Yu and sent his head to Cao Cao, who gave him a proper hero's burial.

Guan Yu, top, holds the Green Dragon. Lu Bei is on the left and Zhang on the right. Silk painting by Japanese artist, Sekkan Sakurai (1715-1790). ⁸⁴

Hua Mulan

Hua Mulan, made famous by the 1998 Disney movie, was a legendary female warrior who disguised herself as a man to take her father's place in the army. Her story challenges traditional gender roles and exemplifies themes of duty and honor. Mulan's name means "magnolia," and the *Ballad of Mulan,* written in the Northern Wei dynasty (386–534 CE) is the source for her ancient tale. The ballad contains only 392 Chinese characters. In Chinese writing, each character usually represents a word, but some only represent sounds; thus, Mulan's tale is a short story.

Nevertheless, it powerfully serves to remind folks that China has heroines. Mulan's ballad of devotion and loyalty to her family centers on the Chinese values of filial piety and patriotism. She was devoted to her parents and her country yet also brave and selfless when facing adversity. Her story reminds us that all have the strength to fulfill their destinies; however, we must cultivate our spirits so we have reserves of courage. Here is Mulan's story.

Mulan sat weaving near the door of her home, sighing. What was she thinking about that made her so gloomy? Was there a boy in her heart?

"No," answered Mulan. "I am not thinking about a boy. There is no boy in my heart. I am melancholy for another reason. Last night, I saw the list of draftees that our emperor has picked to fight for him. My father's name is on the list, yet, he is too old and sick to fight! He has no grown son who can fight in his place. There is only one thing to do. I will buy a horse and go fight in my father's place!"

Mulan headed east and bought a fine warhorse; then she bought a bridle in the south. In the west, she purchased a saddle blanket; in the north, she bought a long whip. Once outfitted, she bid her parents farewell at dawn. She rode all day and arrived at the Yellow River at dusk. She camped that evening next to the river. At sunset, it seemed eerily quiet. All she could hear was the water gently splashing the rocks and the melodious call of the Huà Méi thrush. She was used to her bustling village and the familiar sounds of people calling out to each other in the evening.

At dawn, she left the Yellow River and rode toward the soaring Black Mountains. That night, she camped out again, missing the sounds of her parents calling her. Now, all she heard was the roar of Heishan bandits far away. Mulan continued riding to war for ten thousand miles, flying through mountain passes, with her iron armor gleaming in the sunlight. Finally, she heard the sentry's gong. She had arrived at the battle.

A hundred battles were fought over the next twelve years. Generals and heroes died, rising to meet the Jade Emperor on high, enthroned in the Hall of Brilliance. The Son of Heaven held twelve scrolls listing their merits and gave thousands of rewards. As the war ended, the emperor passed out earthly rewards to the heroes who had survived.

"What do you desire?" the emperor asked Mulan.

"I have no need of a lord's title," she answered. "Just give me a swift horse so I can ride home."

When Mulan's parents heard she had returned, they rushed out to welcome her home. Her younger brother roasted a pig and a sheep to celebrate her return. Mulan rode up with her comrades-in-arms, then left them to go into her room.

"I just want to sit in my chair, take off my war cloak, and put on my old clothes—girl's clothing!" she whispered to herself.

Mulan combed her hair, wove yellow flowers into her braids, and put on makeup. Then, she walked outside into the courtyard to join the men with whom she had fought for twelve years. All that time they thought she was a man.

"Mulan!" the soldiers cried. "We never realized you were a lady!"

Mulan's story led to the saying, "When two deer run together, one can tell the buck from the doe. But when two rabbits run together, how does one know which is the male and which is the female?"

Hua Mulan's return. Mural at Dalongdong Baoan Temple in Taiwan by Pan Li-shui[iii]

Yue Fei

The life journey of Yue Fei (1103-1142 CE) is a symbol of loyalty and patriotism in Chinese culture. His outstanding military campaigns and the tragic turn of events leading to his wrongful execution turned him into a martyr in the eyes of the people. General Yue Fei was renowned for his excellence on the battlefield and his exemplary ethics, especially his patriotism and trustworthiness.

This celebrated general was born in the Northern Song dynasty; however, when he was in his early twenties, Jurchen warriors from northeast China and Russia invaded. They captured the emperor and hundreds of his officials. This forced the Song dynasty, led by the emperor's younger brother, to move south of the Yangtze River, after which it was called the Southern Song.

In his late teens, Yue Fei received military training. People whispered, "Have you seen what he can do? He's superhuman! He can shoot a bow with both his right and left hands! And that's not all. He can draw a bow of four hundred pounds! His spear fighting is unparalleled."

At the time the Jurchens invaded, a dilemma confronted Yue Fei. His father had recently died. He desperately wanted to defend his country from the fierce marauders, yet his absence would leave no one to provide for his mother. He was torn between filial piety and patriotism.

"Yue Fei, take off your shirt," his mother commanded. When Yue Fei bared his back, his mother tattooed four characters: "Jīng zhōng bào guó," or "Serve the country with loyalty."

With his mother's blessing, Yue Fei rode off to fight the Jurchens. He never lost a battle. He once led a small band of 500 men to victory over 100,000 Jurchen soldiers. Yue Fei not only kept the Jurchen at bay but also prevented rival Chinese factions from destroying the Southern Song dynasty.

In addition to his courage and uncanny tactics, Yue Fei was a man of honor. He protected the common people by strictly forbidding his soldiers from looting their farms and villages when passing through. Yet, he also ensured his soldiers had the supplies they needed. He tended them when they were sick. When his soldiers died in battle, he took care of their families. When the emperor rewarded him, he shared the bounty with his men.

Once, Yue Fei squelched a rebellion of citizens unwilling to recognize their new emperor. However, he hesitated when the emperor commanded, "Execute everyone in the city! We have to set an example!"

"Sir!" Yue Fei pleaded. "Surely, we should not kill everyone. Please command me to execute the ringleaders of the rebellion, but spare the ordinary people. Then, they will be thankful for your mercy and loyal to you forever."

The emperor agreed to Yue Fei's suggestion. "Yue Fei, you are shrewd! I appreciate your loyalty to me and your care for the people's welfare."

Yet, Yue Fei had enemies. His popularity with the emperor and his soldiers made them jealous. They whispered to the emperor, "Yue Fei is a long way from your capital. He's getting too powerful. The local people are devoted to him. What's keeping him from instigating his own rebellion against you?"

The emperor recalled Yue Fei, who was at the cusp of retaking Kaifeng from the Jurchens. Kaifeng was China's largest and most prosperous city at the time. Yue Fei obediently returned but remarked, "I spent ten years securing this territory from the Jurchen invaders. When I leave, they'll grab it back in a flash."

When Yue Fei arrived at the capital, his enemies at court convinced the emperor to revoke his position as general. Months later, they presented trumped-up charges, and Yue Fei, still in his thirties, was sentenced to die. Legend says that after his death, black mist swirled through the sky.

Statue of Yue Fei at his tomb and shrine in Hangzhou [86]

Chapter 9: Mountains and Rivers: Magical Landscapes

Natural landscapes hold a prominent role in Chinese folklore. Mountains and rivers are not just physical features; they are imbued with spiritual significance and magical qualities. In the Chinese worldview, the natural world impacts human life. Mountains are the home of gods, spirits, and sages. Medicinal plants grow on mountains, and pilgrims travel to mountains to meditate and seek enlightenment. Since mountains are sacred, most mountains in China have small shrines, and many have temples and monasteries.

Rivers bring life, change, and nourishment. Chinese civilization emerged in the fertile regions along the Yellow and Yangtze rivers, foundational pillars of Chinese culture. The Chinese called the Yellow River their "Mother River" but also "China's Sorrow." Rivers enable transportation and irrigation for farming, but they are also agents of chaos when they flood. In Chinese folklore, rivers are home to water spirits and sometimes even dragons.

Mount Tai, in eastern China's Shandong Province, stands five thousand feet high and is one of China's Five Sacred Mountains. The ancient Chinese considered it a holy place where emperors would perform rituals to ensure the country's prosperity and peace. In Chinese legends, it served as a meeting point between the divine and the earthly. As the eastern-most mountain of the Five Sacred Mountains, Mount Tai represented birth, renewal, and the sunrise.

Chinese emperors traveled to Mount Tai to offer the Feng Shan sacrifices of food and jade items. At the foot of the mountain, the emperor honored Earth, and at the mountaintop, he honored Heaven. The sacrifices enabled the emperor to receive the Mandate of Heaven. Even Japan, Korea, and states in Central Asia sent representatives to attend the Feng Shan sacrifices in the Tang dynasty.

The "Great Deity of Mount Tai" was the **Dongyue Emperor**, the mountain's supreme god. He was also the god of the underworld, deciding how long each human should live. His wife (or daughter) was Bixia Yuanjun, the "Goddess of the Blue Dawn" or the "Heavenly Jade Lady." She was the deity of destiny and childbirth.

The Dongyue Emperor was not always a god. At one time, he was Prince Wucheng of the Shang dynasty (1600–1046 BCE) serving in King Zhou's court. King Zhou was infatuated with his concubine named Daji. He failed to realize Daji was not really a woman but a fox spirit (húlí jīng). Fox spirits, or vixen spirits, could shapeshift. They had nine tails; eight extended from the main tail. Some fox spirits were benevolent spirits, and others were evil. Daji was an evil húlí jīng.

A vixen spirit from a Chinese tomb mural, late fourth to mid-fifth century CE [87]

King Zhou always had abysmal character, but after consorting with Daji, he worsened. He cruelly tortured his ministers who dared suggest a different opinion. The king became enamored with Prince Wucheng's wife, Lady Jia, and tried to violate her. She committed suicide rather than submit to his advances. Wucheng's sister Huang was another concubine of the despicable king. When she heard what happened to Lady Jia, she scolded King Zhou, and he angrily threw her from his tower window to her death.

After his wife and sister died at King Zhou's hands, Prince Wucheng defected to the rival state of Zhou, where King Wu was trying to topple the Shang dynasty. Wu eventually won the war and established the new Zhou dynasty. However, Prince Wucheng died in the Battle of Muye, which brought the ultimate victory. For avenging unrighteousness, Heaven appointed him as the Dongyue Emperor, supreme leader over the gods of the Five Sacred Mountains.

The **Legend of the White Snake** is one of China's most endearing love stories. It centers on a young man named Xu Xian and a white snake spirit named Bai Suzhen (Lady Bai). Lady Bai was once a malevolent demon, but she reformed and spent one thousand years studying the principles of Tao on Mount Emei. The Dragon King of the East China Sea changed her into a woman, although she could still shapeshift into a snake.

Lady Bai's next goal was to earn immortality through good deeds, and she became a disciple of Lishan Laomu, the Tao goddess of Mount Li. One day, Lady Bai saw a beggar hitting a green snake with a club and intervened, saving the snake. The green snake promised to stay with Lady Bai forever, so she nicknamed the snake Qingmei, meaning "green sister."

Later, Lady Bai traveled to West Lake in Hangzhou. On Tomb Sweeping Day, she met a man named Xu Xian at the Broken Bridge. She recognized him from a past life—he had rescued her from a deadly danger. Xu Xian and Lady Bai fell in love, married, and had a baby boy. Yet, trouble soon erupted. A Buddhist monk named Fahai recognized Lady Bai's true identity.

"Your wife is not a true human. She's a snake spirit!"

"You're insane! My wife isn't a snake; she's a woman!" Xu Xian protested.

"If you don't believe me, test it out," Fahai said. "Dragon Boat Festival is coming up. Have her drink realgar wine. See what happens."

(Realgar is an arsenic sulfide mineral that the Chinese traditionally mixed into their wine at the Dragon Boat Festival. They believed it drove away evil spirits, illnesses, and insects.)

Xu Xian gave Lady Bai some realgar wine at the Dragon Boat Festival, and she suddenly morphed into a large white snake.

"Ahhhh!" screamed Xu Xian. He had a heart attack and died on the spot.

"Oh, my darling! You can't die!" Lady Bai cried. She flew to Mount Emei, where a special fungus called lingzhi grew. She hurried back to her husband and used the immortal fungus to revive him.

"Lady Bai, I still love you, even if you are a snake," gasped Xu Xian. Lady Bai embraced and kissed him, but she knew the danger was not over. The monk Fahai was still out there.

She was right. Fahai came after Lady Bai, captured her, and locked her in the Leifeng Pagoda in Hangzhou. Xu Xian searched all over China for his wife. When he heard she was imprisoned at the Leifeng Pagoda, he traveled there and tried to free her, but Fahai's sorcery was too strong. Xu Xian became a monk at the nearby monastery so he could stay close to his wife. He gave baby Xu Shilin to Qingmei, his wife's green snake friend. Xu Shilin grew up to be a scholar and finally rescued his mother from the Leifeng Pagoda.

A wood carving of Lady Bai at the Leifeng Pagoda on Sunset Mountain[88]

Another Chinese folktale about a mountain is **Emperor Qin Shi Huang's Search for Mount Penglai**. Qin Shi Huang was the first emperor of the Qin dynasty (221-206 BCE), and he was obsessed with immortality.

"How can I live forever? What must I do?" he persistently asked.

One of his ministers rubbed his beard. "I have heard stories about Mount Penglai. It is a white spirit mountain in the center of the sea where eight immortals live in a splendid palace. Legend says that the fruit growing on the magical island trees can heal all diseases, make a person forever young, and even revive the dead."

The emperor leaned forward with excitement. "Xu Fu!" he called to his court sorcerer. "Take ten exquisite ships and five hundred children. Choose the handsomest boys and the most beautiful girls. Sail across the Eastern Sea until you find the magical white mountain, then bring me the fruit of immortality."

Why did Emperor Qin send five hundred children? Perhaps they were to colonize the heavenly island. Sorcerer Xu Fu found a large island with a high, snow-covered mountain. (It might have been Mount Fuji on Japan's Honshu Island.) However, he could not find the fruit of immortality, so he sailed back to China. Later, he sailed east again but never returned. Emperor Qin fell into despair, searching desperately for another way to live forever.

A painting of one of the ships sent to find the Island of Immortality [89]

Rivers, home to water spirits and the occasional dragon, featured in many Chinese folktales. One was the story of **Lady Meng Jiang**. Meng Jiang and her husband, Qi Liang, were newlyweds and hoping to start a family. However, the emperor had started a project to renovate and add on to the Great Wall of China. Since the wall was over 13,000 miles long, the emperor needed a million men to do the work. Meng Jiang's husband was among the many the emperor drafted to labor on the wall.

Meng Jiang stayed at home, worrying about Qi Liang. After many months, some men in their town returned from their duty on the wall, but her husband was not among them. She was horrified when she heard about the conditions the men worked under.

"We were lucky to survive," the men told her. "Never enough food. Many men died of starvation or were worked to death. The wall is mostly in the mountains, and it is cold for much of the year. Then, the landslides swept some workers away. Leopards and bears preyed on us."

Meng Jiang fretted. "My poor husband, working so hard with little food."

That night, she had a nightmare in which she saw her husband at the wall. "Meng Jiang!" he cried. "I'm so cold!"

Meng Jiang awakened and determined to travel to her husband. "Winter is coming soon. I must go to Qi Liang! I'll take warm clothing and food."

She traveled to the wall, but when she got there, she had difficulty finding the section on which her husband was working. Finally, she met some other men from her region.

"Brothers!" she cried. "Where is my husband?"

They looked at her sadly. "Little sister, Qi Liang died."

"No!" wailed Meng Jiang. "Where is he buried?"

"Oh, little sister, we don't even know. You see, the wall is actually two parallel walls, built of stone or brick. We fill in the middle with rubble, rocks, and packed earth. When one of us dies, we just lay him in that middle section and cover him with rubble and dirt. Countless men are buried within the wall's structure. We are so sorry."

Meng Jiang flung herself to the ground next to the wall, weeping. Her piercing wails were so loud that the earth shook, and a section of the wall crumbled. The construction workers fled, snatching up Meng Jiang and escaping the falling bricks and stones. When the dust settled, Meng Jiang peered at the wall.

"Look! Among that rubble! See those bones? Could they be my husband's?"

"Maybe," the men said. "That is the area where we buried Qi Liang. But we buried several other men with him."

"I'll prick my finger and let the blood drip on the bones. My blood will only penetrate my husband's bones!"

Thus, Lady Meng Jiang identified her husband's remains and gave him a proper burial with the usual rites. Meanwhile, the emperor, who had been inspecting work on the Great Wall, reached the section where Qi Liang died. He heard about how Lady Meng Jiang's wails caused the wall to collapse, exposing her husband's bones.

"What a story!" remarked the emperor. "I must meet this woman!"

When they brought Lady Meng Jiang to meet him, he was awestruck by her beauty.

"Marry me, Lady Meng!"

"But you already have several wives and dozens of concubines."

"I know, but none of them has your strength of character."

"Well," Meng Jiang answered. "I'll marry you if you do three things."

"Anything! Just name them!"

"First, you must order a forty-nine-day festival to honor my husband. I must properly mourn him before I can marry again. Second, you and all your officials must attend the festival. You need to honor all the thousands of men who have died working on your project. Third, you must build a forty-nine-foot-high terrace over the river. I will stand on it to offer a sacrifice to my husband."

"Yes! Yes! I'll do all three things," the emperor eagerly answered.

At the end of the forty-nine-day festival, Lady Meng Jiang climbed to the top of the platform over the river. She turned to the emperor. "My sacrifice is myself! I'm going to join my husband!"

At that, Meng Jiang leaped into the river and drowned.

A section of the Great Wall in the mountains[40]

The **Xiang River Goddesses** were once princesses, the daughters of the legendary Emperor Yao. Their names were E Huang (Fairy Radiance) and Nu Ying (Maiden Bloom). Emperor Yao ruled over the Yellow River Valley in northeastern China during the 2200s BCE. "History" from this era is more likely to be folktales, as China did not develop writing for another thousand years. Yao was the emperor at the beginning of China's Great Flood.

In those days, China's rulers were not hereditary. The king chose a leader to succeed him based on merit, not kinship. Emperor Yao chose one of his ministers, Shun, to inherit his throne. He handed the throne over to Shun years before he died because he had failed to control the devastating, years-long flooding. By this time, Emperor Yao had given his daughters E Huang and Nu Ying in marriage to Shun.

The young ladies loved their husband and had a good relationship with each other. When they were newly married and Shun was not yet king, the sisters heard that Shun's evil father, stepmother, and half-brother were plotting to murder him. The morally bankrupt trio wanted to steal the dowry of sheep, cattle, and grain that Emperor Yao had given Shun. E Huang and Nu Ying warned their new husband and gave him a magical bird coat for protection. Shun's father told him to go up on the barn to mend the roof. Once he was up there, they set the barn on fire and took the ladder away. However, wearing his magical bird coat, Shun flew safely to the ground.

Shun's despicable relatives then threw him into a well to drown. However, the sisters had anticipated this and given him a magic dragon coat. He swam underwater through a conduit leading to the well and escaped. Next, the sisters bathed their husband in a magic antidote, which thwarted another murder attempt by his homicidal family. Finally, Emperor Yao removed Shun and his wives from the bloodthirsty family and brought them to court.

Shun eventually became the emperor, and all went well. He offered sacrifices to Shang Di, the Supreme God, then offered burnt offerings at China's sacred mountains. He also offered sacrifices to the Yellow River and Yangtze River. Yu the Engineer stopped the flooding that was devastating the realm, and Shun appointed him as his successor.

E Huang and Nu Ying [41]

Then, after Shun was emperor for fifty years, disaster struck. He was on a military expedition against the Miao near the headwaters of the Xiang River. He missed his footing, fell into the water, and the raging current swept him away, never to be seen again. His two wives rushed to the region, desperately searching for their husband, to no avail. As E Huang and Nu Ying sat by the river weeping, their tears stained the bamboo shoots. To this day, the bamboo in that area has spots. Finally, the two sisters flung themselves into the river to join their husband in death. They reincarnated as the Xiang River goddesses, the subject of Chinese poetry for millennia.

Chapter 10: Magical Lanterns and Chinese Festivals

Chinese folklore often explains the reason behind Chinese festivals. Other times, the stories take place during a key festival. China's Lantern Festival marks the end of the two-week Chinese New Year celebration. Red lanterns adorn the streets, symbolizing auspicious fortune and driving away malevolent spirits. This chapter unravels the mythology behind the lanterns. Another key celebration featuring lanterns is the Mid-Autumn Festival, and we'll explore how and why it is observed.

A Qing dynasty rank badge with a crane motif "

One popular folktale that explains the origin of the Lantern Festival is the **Legend of the Jade Emperor's Crane**. In this story, the Jade Emperor had a favorite celestial crane that adorned his heavenly palace garden. One day, the crane flew from Heaven down to Earth, where he foraged for germinating seeds and sprouted plants next to a village. Not realizing he was the Jade Emperor's crane, the villagers killed him because he was harming their crops.

When the Jade Emperor found out what had happened to his crane, his anger erupted. "I shall send a massive fire to destroy this village on the fifteenth day of the first lunar month!"

However, one of the Jade Emperor's seven daughters flew down to Earth to warn the villagers of the impending inferno.

"What can we do?" the villagers wondered. "How can we avoid the fire?"

They visited Shèngrén, a wise old man who lived in a nearby village.

Shèngrén threw some dàmá leaves on a brazier and pondered the perplexing problem as he breathed in the smoke. His brow furrowed as the villagers looked on anxiously. Finally, he brightened.

"Trick the Jade Emperor!" he advised. "Make him think your village is already going up in smoke."

"How?" asked the villagers.

"For three days, burn enormous bonfires in the streets. Don't forget to set off firecrackers and light red lanterns. Do this on the fifteenth day of the first lunar month and for two days prior."

The villagers followed Shèngrén's advice. When the Jade Emperor's celestial soldiers arrived to immolate the village, they saw billowing black smoke and flames leaping up from various points of the village. They heard explosions, and the entire village glowed red from the burning lanterns.

"Someone has done our work for us!" the troops laughed as they gazed at the spectacular display. "An enemy tribe must have attacked them."

They flew back to Heaven and reported to the Jade Emperor that the village was already destroyed. Back on Earth, the villagers breathed a sigh of relief. Each year, they celebrated their narrow escape by lighting red lanterns, setting off fireworks, and burning bonfires. Some brave souls even leaped over the fires. The village's annual tradition spread throughout the land until all of China celebrated it.

Chinese red lanterns [48]

Another tale about the Chinese red lanterns, **Laozu and the Nian Monster**, casts the Jade Emperor in a more benevolent, protective light. He passed a heavenly decree for the people to use red lanterns to protect themselves from a mythical beast called a nian. This creature lived inside mountains or under the sea. However, its name is the same as the Chinese word for "year." The ancient Chinese believed it came out of the sea or mountains at the new year. The Chinese phrase "guònián" means "pass (celebrate) the new year," but it can also carry the meaning of getting the nian monster to pass or leave.

At New Year (in January or February, depending on the Chinese lunar calendar), the nian was ravenous and ready to eat. In the dead of winter, food was hard to find in the wild, so it would come into villages or towns. It raided food stores, ate the village dogs and chickens, and even ate people, especially children. The nian's head looked like a lion with a flat face and long fangs. Its body was more like a dog.

The beast disliked fire, the color red, and loud noise, so people banged drums, set off firecrackers, lit bonfires, wore red clothing, and hung red banners and red lanterns everywhere. They left food outside the house for the beast so it would not eat people. At the Chinese New Year, two men put on a lion costume and performed the lion dance to the sound of drums and gongs. The lion dance chased away evil spirits and the nian monster. It brought luck and prosperity to the new year.

A Taoist monk named Hongjun Laozu tricked the nian monster. He climbed up the mountain where the nian lived and found it in a cave.

"Nian," he said, "I am a peaceful monk. I mean you no harm. But I want you to stop eating people. Stop frightening them. Let them enjoy celebrating the New Year."

The nian laughed. "Haha! You've come into my lair. Thank you for delivering my food today. I'll enjoy eating you."

"Oh, but I'm just an old man," remarked Hongjun. "I'm not delicious. Tell me, do you eat the poisonous snakes living on this mountain?"

"Of course!" sneered the tian. "Let me show you."

The monster left the cave, gathered up some snakes, and ate them. When it got back to the cave, Hongjun asked, "What about those wild beasts lurking on the back of the mountain? Are you powerful enough to tame them?"

"Certainly!" replied the nian. It left for a while, then returned. "The wild beasts all bowed to me. Now, I am going to eat you!"

"I understand," said the monk. "But let me remove my tunic and robe. They won't taste very good."

Hongjun threw off his robe and tunic, exposing his red undergarments. Terrified of the color red, the nian monster ran to the back of its cave. "Go away! Go away! I can't bear to look at your red underwear!"

"No! I will not go away," said Hongjun sternly. "However, I will put my tunic and robe back on so you don't have to look at the red underclothes. But you must let me ride on your back."

"Okay! Okay! Just cover that red!"

Hongjun climbed on the tian monster's back and rode it into the town. "Dear people, you do not have to be afraid of the tian monster anymore," he announced. "He hates the color red, so just hang red banners and lanterns and paste red paper on your doors. The nian will not bother you."

The people followed Hongjun's advice, and that is why people wear red and cover their homes and streets with red lanterns and banners at the Chinese New Year. Hongjun also told them that the monster hated loud noise, so they set off firecrackers and created the lion dance to the deafening sound of drums and clanging cymbals.

Lion dance "

Another folktale explaining the origins of the Lantern Festival is the story of a girl named **Yuan Xiao**, which took place in the Han dynasty. Yuan Xiao, a young maid in the palace, was homesick for her family. As the Chinese New Year approached, Yuan Xiao grew increasingly depressed. The New Year celebration had always been a large family affair, with all the extended family—cousins, aunts, uncles—gathering at the ancestral village where her grandmother and grandfather lived.

"Now, I am all by myself. When will I ever see my family again?" Yuan Xiao wept as she sat next to a well, where she had come to draw water. "I want to jump into that well. What is the point of living without my family?"

She heard a man clearing his throat behind her. It was Dongfang Shuo, a palace official who had always been kind to her.

"Yuan Xiao, I am so sorry that you are missing your family at the new year." Dongfang Shuo said kindly. "I think I can help you reunite with your loved ones."

"Really?" Is that possible?" Yuan Xiao asked, wiping the tears from her cheeks.

"I have a plan. I think it will work. It's quite clever, really," Dongfang Shuo said, smiling.

The next day, another maid came running in to where Yuan Xiao was working. "Did you hear the news? Dongfang Shuo opened a fortune-telling booth in the market!"

"Dongfang Shuo? Telling the future? Does he have the gift?"

"Apparently," answered Yuan Xiao's co-worker. "He's saying that fire will destroy our city on the fifteenth day of the first lunar month."

"That's next week!" Yuan Xiao exclaimed. "I wonder what the emperor will do?"

The emperor had already called Dongfang Shuo in for a consultation. "How can I prevent this disaster?" he asked.

"The entire city needs to make offerings to the fire god," answered Dongfang Shuo. "Set off fireworks! Hang red lanterns and make yuanxiao (rice dumplings). Maybe the fire god will spare our city."

On the emperor's orders, everyone prepared for the festival. Yuan Xiao made the yuanxiao for everyone in the palace. That night, Dongfang Shuo led Yuan Xiao and other palace employees through the city filled with fireworks, red banners, and bright red lanterns. Crowds of people were enjoying the sights while eating rice dumplings. Suddenly, Yuan Xiao heard someone call her name.

"Yuan Xiao! Look, everyone. It's Yuan Xiao! Our daughter is here!"

Yuan Xiao peered through the smoke from the firecrackers. It was her family!

"Mama! Baba! Oh, and here's Granny and Grandpa! Sister! Brother! Oh, I have missed all of you so much!"

Yuan Xiao embraced her family. "Daughter," her father explained. "We came into the city to enjoy the celebration. It was a long way to travel, but we were also hoping to see you! Heaven has answered our prayers!"

Yuan Xiao turned to Dongfang Shuo. "Thank you, kind sir, for reuniting me with my family!"

At that moment, the emperor walked up. "Dongfang Shuo, this celebration has been a splendid success! I believe we have satisfied the fire god!" At that, the emperor winked at his minister. "Everyone is enjoying themselves, and families are reuniting. I decree that this festival of red lanterns and rice dumplings shall be an annual affair. We'll celebrate the fifteenth day after the first full moon of the year and name the festival after this young lady, Yuan Xiao! Her rice dumplings are the best I have ever eaten!"

The Moon Festival, also known as China's **Mid-Autumn Festival**, falls on the fifteenth day of the eighth month in the Chinese lunar calendar. In the Gregorian calendar, it is in late September or early October. One of China's oldest festivals, it is a harvest celebration that also celebrates the moon, which appears at its brightest this time of year. It is also a time to worship the moon goddess, Chang'e.

An image from the Luna spacecraft of the rabbit on the moon "

We learned in chapter two how Chang'e, the subject of many Chinese poems, got to the moon. She is sometimes called "Chang Xi," and one of China's oldest preserved texts, *Classics of Mountains and Seas*, writes of her bathing the moon. *Journey to the West* says Chang'e lived in "Guǎng Han Hong," or a cold, vast palace on the moon. Chang'e's pet, the Jade Rabbit, accompanied her to the moon. When the Chinese looked at the moon, they saw the image of the rabbit pounding herbs on a mortar for the immortals.

Journey to the West tells the story of how the Monkey King was fighting a demoness one day. Taiyin Xingjun, sometimes considered a manifestation of Chang'e, came down to Earth on a colored cloud. "Monkey King! The demon you are fighting is really my Jade Rabbit, she said. "She guards my palace on the moon, but she escaped, and it has been a year since I last saw her. Please spare her for my sake. I will take her back to the moon, and she will bother no one here on Earth."

The Monkey King reluctantly agreed, and Taiyin Xingjun took her rabbit back to the moon and gave it plenty of work to keep it busy.

At the Mid-Autumn Festival, the Chinese people celebrate the rice and wheat harvest by offering food and burning incense to the moon and praying to it. Families and friends gather outdoors to gaze at the moon, which symbolizes harmony. They eat mooncakes—dense, round pastries with a filling inside. Children have fun guessing what filling is in the mooncake. Is it sweet like lotus bean paste, or does it have a salted duck egg inside?

Dragon and lion dances are performed, and the ubiquitous red lanterns light the streets, symbolizing good fortune, happiness, and prosperity. One version of the story of Chang'e says that she and her husband were permitted to reunite once a year on the full moon of the eighth lunar month. The red lanterns lit the way for Chang'e on her journey back to her husband.

Conclusion

Chinese folktales open a window into Chinese culture and values. The themes and motifs presented in these chapters explore the interplay of history, mythology, and cultural identity. These tales of gods, heroes, magical creatures, and ordinary people impart moral lessons across generations. The stories reflect the deep-rooted philosophies that have permeated Chinese culture for thousands of years.

Several of these stories are macabre and brutal. Others are cloyingly sentimental. Some may be difficult to decipher from a Western mindset. Yet, together, they shed light on the soul of China, offering endless insights and inspiration. At first glance, some stories may seem simple, yet they convey deeper, symbolic morals. They explain how the world began, reinforce cultural traditions, and teach what is right and prudent through quintessential characters.

Many tales reflect Taoist, Buddhist, and Confucian values that still permeate China's culture. For instance, filial piety—the reverence, obedience, and concern for one's parents, older siblings, and elderly family members—shines through. Proper social hierarchy, especially within the family, is paramount in Chinese culture to this day.

Other religious and cultural values woven into these stories include Chinese concepts of immortality, balance, and integrity. The principle of yin and yang, representing opposing yet interrelated forces that embody balance and duality, serves as a foundational element in many Chinese folktales. Yin and yang are obvious in the primordial egg story yet quietly pervade the tale of the Herdsman and the Weaver Goddess—one from Earth and one from Heaven.

Several stories explore the pursuit of immortality through enlightenment and self-cultivation. Other tales teach moral values like honesty and humility. The story of Hui and the Golden Pheasant illustrates that dreams really can come true and that good intentions are worthy. The Monkey King tales emphasize that pride comes before a fall, yet tenacity and loyalty can save the day. Dashed hopes, realized dreams, magic, adventures, and cultural values—Chinese folktales have it all.

Here's another book by Enthralling History that you might like

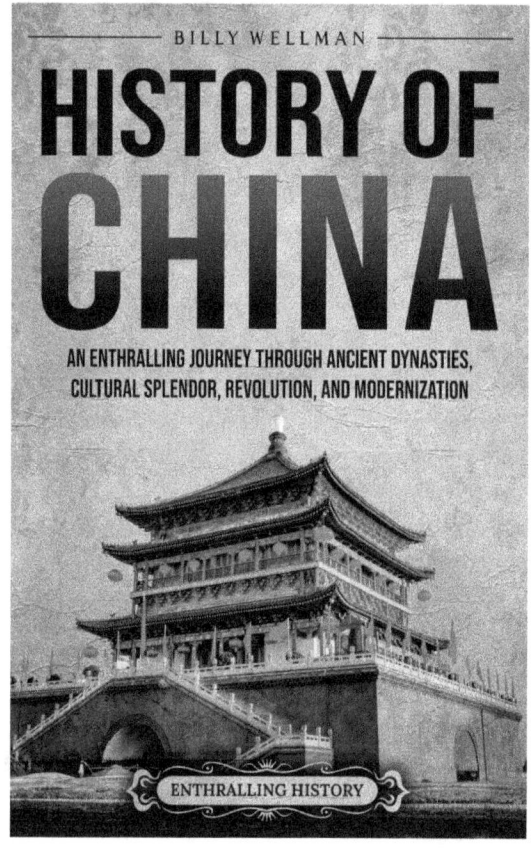

Free limited time bonus

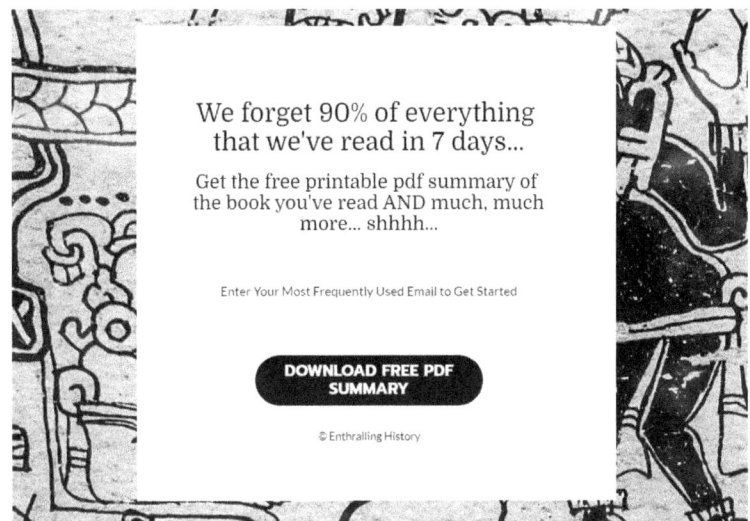

Stop for a moment. We have a free bonus set up for you. The problem is this: we forget 90% of everything that we read after 7 days. Crazy fact, right? Here's the solution: we've created a printable, 1-page pdf summary for this book that you're reading now. All you have to do to get your free pdf summary is to go to the following website:
https://livetolearn.lpages.co/enthrallinghistory/

Or, Scan the QR code!

Once you do, it will be intuitive. Enjoy, and thank you!

Bibliography

Cutter, Robert Joe. *The Poetry of Cao Zhi*. De Gruyter, 2021.

Fu, Shelley, and Patrick Yee. *Chinese Myths and Legends: The Monkey King and Other Adventures*. Tuttle Publishing, 2018.

Hamilton, Mae. "Chinese God Pangu." *Mythopedia*. Accessed July 17, 2025. https://mythopedia.com/topics/pangu/.

Hamilton, Mae. "Chinese Goddess Nuwa." *Mythopedia*. Accessed July 17, 2025. https://mythopedia.com/topics/nuwa/.

Huang, Dehai. *Illustrated Myths & Legends of China: The Ages of Chaos and Heroes*. Shanghai Press, 2018.

Legge, James. *The Notions of the Chinese Concerning Gods and Spirits*. Hong Kong Register, 1852.

Ling, Vivian, Peng Wang, and Yang Xi. *A Bilingual Treasury of Chinese Folktales: Ten Traditional Stories in Chinese and English*. Tuttle Publishing, 2022.

Ling, Vivian, Peng Wang, and Yang Xi. *Chinese Stories for Language Learners: A Treasury of Proverbs and Folktales in Chinese and English*. Tuttle Publishing, 2019.

Macgowan, J. *Chinese Folklore Tales*. Macmillan and Co., Limited, 1910. https://www.worldoftales.com/Chinese_folktales.html#gsc.tab=0.

Nunes, Shiho S., and Lak-Khee Tay-Audouard. *Chinese Folktales: The Dragon Slayer and Other Timeless Tales*. Tuttle Publishing, 2021.

Personal Salvation and Filial Piety: Two Precious Scroll Narratives of Guanyin and Her Acolytes. Translated by Wilt L. Idema. University of Hawaii Press, 2008.

Pitman, Norman Hinsdale. *A Chinese Wonder Book.* E. P. Dutton & Co., 1919. https://www.worldoftales.com/Chinese_folktales.html#gsc.tab=0.

Selection from the Lotus Sutra: "The Daughter of the Dragon King." Asia for Educators: Columbia University, 1999. Accessed August 2, 2025. https://afe.easia.columbia.edu/ps/cup/lotus_sutra_dragon_king.pdf.

Sima Qian, *Shiji, Records of the Grand Scribe.* China Knowledge: An Encyclopaedia on Chinese History and Literature, 2010. Accessed March 13, 2025. http://www.chinaknowledge.de/Literature/Historiography/shiji.html.

The Ballad of Mulan: A Rhyming Translation. Translated by Evan Mantyk. The Society of Classical Poets, 2020. Accessed September 1, 2025. https://classicalpoets.org/2018/09/the-ballad-of-mulan-a-rhyming-translation/.

The Works of Motze. Confucius Publications, 1980.

Wilhelm, R., Norman Hinsdale Pitman, and Andrew Lang, eds. *Chinese Fairy Tales, Folktales and Fables.* Accessed July 15, 2025. https://fairytalez.com/region/chinese/#google_vignette.

Wu, Cheng'en. *Monkey: Journey to the West.* Translated by Arthur Waley. Penguin Classics, 1994.

Wu, Qinglong, Zhijun Zhao, Li Liu, et al. "Outburst Flood at 1920 BCE Supports Historicity of China's successful Flood and the Xia Dynasty." *Science* 353, no. 6299 (2016): 10.1126/science.aaf084 https://www.science.org/doi/10.1126/science.aaf0842.

"Yellow Emperor." *China Daily.com.* March 12, 2012. Accessed July 17, 2025. https://www.chinadaily.com.cn/life/yellow_emperor_memorial_ceremony/2012-03/12/content_14812971.htm.

Image Sources

1 RootOfAllLight, CC BY-SA 4.0 <https://creativecommons.org/licenses/by-sa/4.0>, via Wikimedia Commons: https://commons.wikimedia.org/wiki/File:Qilin.svg
2 https://commons.wikimedia.org/wiki/File:Anonymous-Fuxi_and_N%C3%BCwa.jpg
3 Gary Todd, CC0, via Wikimedia Commons: https://commons.wikimedia.org/wiki/File:Huangdi_Temple_-_Statue_of_Huangdi,_the_%22Yellow_Emperor%22.jpg
4 https://commons.wikimedia.org/wiki/File:Court_ladies_pounding_silk_from_a_painting_(%E6%8D%A3%E7%BB%83%E5%9B%BE)_by_Emperor_Huizong.jpg
5 https://commons.wikimedia.org/wiki/File:%E7%8E%89%E7%9A%87%E5%A4%A7%E5%B8%9D%E7%95%AB%E5%83%8F.jpg
6 https://commons.wikimedia.org/wiki/File:Chang%27e_flees_to_the_moon_by_Tsukioka_Yoshitoshi.jpg
7 ScribblingGeek, CC BY-SA 4.0 <https://creativecommons.org/licenses/by-sa/4.0>, via Wikimedia Commons: https://commons.wikimedia.org/wiki/File:Zhao_Gongming_Caishen.jpg
8 Rolf Müller (User:Rolfmueller), CC BY-SA 3.0 <http://creativecommons.org/licenses/by-sa/3.0/>, via Wikimedia Commons: https://commons.wikimedia.org/wiki/File:Fourheavenlykings4096x1360.jpg
9 https://commons.wikimedia.org/wiki/File:1962-01_1962%E5%B9%B4_%E6%B5%99%E6%B1%9F%E7%BB%8D%E5%89%A7_%E5%AD%99%E6%82%9F%E7%A9%BA.jpg

10 en:User:Wikiality123, CC BY-SA 3.0 <http://creativecommons.org/licenses/by-sa/3.0/>, via Wikimedia Commons; https://commons.wikimedia.org/wiki/File:Silk_Route_extant.JPG

11 VK Cheong, CC BY-SA 3.0 <https://creativecommons.org/licenses/by-sa/3.0>, via Wikimedia Commons: https://commons.wikimedia.org/wiki/File:Tang_-_Ferghana_War_Horse.JPG

12 https://commons.wikimedia.org/wiki/File:Flag_of_China_(1889%E2%80%931912).svg

13 https://commons.wikimedia.org/wiki/File:Xuanzang_w.jpg

14 https://commons.wikimedia.org/wiki/File:Eleven-Headed_Guanyin_(1943.57.14).jpg

15 https://commons.wikimedia.org/wiki/File:JourneytotheWest.jpg#file

16 Daftation, CC BY-SA 4.0 <https://creativecommons.org/licenses/by-sa/4.0>, via Wikimedia Commons: https://commons.wikimedia.org/wiki/File:Sacred_Lotus_in_a_Pond_2.jpg

17 https://commons.wikimedia.org/wiki/File:Eight_Immortals_Crossing_the_Sea_-_Project_Gutenberg_eText_15250.jpg

18 https://commons.wikimedia.org/wiki/File:Album_of_18_Daoist_Paintings_-_10.jpg

19 Collectie Wereldmuseum (v/h Tropenmuseum), part of the National Museum of World Cultures, CC BY-SA 3.0 <https://creativecommons.org/licenses/by-sa/3.0>, via Wikimedia Commons: https://commons.wikimedia.org/wiki/File:COLLECTIE_TROPENMUSEUM_Zilveren_Manjusri_beeld_afkomstig_uit_Ngemplak_Semongan_TMnr_10016132.jpg

20 Photo Dharma from Sadao, Thailand, CC BY 2.0 <https://creativecommons.org/licenses/by/2.0>, via Wikimedia Commons: https://commons.wikimedia.org/wiki/File:011_Long_Nu_(9212414791).jpg

21 atgu, CC BY-SA 3.0 <https://creativecommons.org/licenses/by-sa/3.0>, via Wikimedia Commons: https://commons.wikimedia.org/wiki/File:Brand_-_panoramio.jpg

22 Mary Harrsch from Springfield, Oregon, USA, CC BY 2.0 <https://creativecommons.org/licenses/by/2.0>, via Wikimedia Commons: https://commons.wikimedia.org/wiki/File:Detail_from_plaque_depicting_the_Dragon_Boat_Festival_Cloisonne_enamel_1735-1795_Qing_dynasty_China_(3)_(253364827).jpg

23 Metropolitan Museum of Art, CC0, via Wikimedia Commons: https://commons.wikimedia.org/wiki/File:MET_TR.457.2012_image0002_(Moving_Chinese_dragon).jpg

24 Metropolitan Museum of Art, CC0, via Wikimedia Commons: https://commons.wikimedia.org/wiki/File:MET_30_75_5_d1.jpeg

25 User:Vmenkov, CC BY-SA 3.0 <http://creativecommons.org/licenses/by-sa/3.0/>, via Wikimedia Commons: https://commons.wikimedia.org/wiki/File:Hokkien-Huay-Kuan-2330.jpg

26 Isidijeron, CC BY-SA 4.0 <https://creativecommons.org/licenses/by-sa/4.0>, via Wikimedia Commons: https://commons.wikimedia.org/wiki/File:Nezha_contra_Ao_Guang.jpg

27 https://commons.wikimedia.org/wiki/File:Ke_Jiusi-Twin_Bamboo.jpg

28 https://commons.wikimedia.org/wiki/File:Birds,_bamboo,_and_camelias_-_Google_Art_Project.jpg

29 https://commons.wikimedia.org/wiki/File:Dog_by_bamboo.jpg

30 User:Vmenkov, CC BY-SA 3.0 <https://creativecommons.org/licenses/by-sa/3.0>, via Wikimedia Commons: https://commons.wikimedia.org/wiki/File:Xiao_Xiu_-_NE_turtle_-_P1070560.JPG

31 https://commons.wikimedia.org/wiki/File:Yu_Sheng_-_Fenghuang_-_18th-century.jpg

32 https://commons.wikimedia.org/wiki/File:Twelve_Symbols_national_emblem_of_China.svg

33 Anonyme, CC0, via Wikimedia Commons: https://commons.wikimedia.org/wiki/File:Ph%C3%A9nix_ou_Fong_Hoang_pos%C3%A9_sur_un_rocher,_J_873(5).jpg

34 https://commons.wikimedia.org/wiki/File:Three_Brothers_edit.jpg#file

35 姜 明雄, CC0, via Wikimedia Commons: https://commons.wikimedia.org/wiki/File:DSC07682_(30723853208).jpg

36 Morio, CC BY-SA 4.0 <https://creativecommons.org/licenses/by-sa/4.0>, via Wikimedia Commons: https://commons.wikimedia.org/wiki/File:Yue_Fei_statue_(Zhonglieci)_5_2016_January.jpg

37 https://commons.wikimedia.org/wiki/File:Yanju%27s_tomb,_nine-tailed_fox.jpg

38 Jakub Hałun, CC BY-SA 3.0 <https://creativecommons.org/licenses/by-sa/3.0>, via Wikimedia Commons: https://commons.wikimedia.org/wiki/File:20090524_Hangzhou_7423.jpg

39 https://commons.wikimedia.org/wiki/File:La_expedici%C3%B3n_de_Xu_Fu,_por_Utagawa_Kuniyoshi.jpg

40 Luca Casartelli, CC BY-SA 2.0 <https://creativecommons.org/licenses/by-sa/2.0>, via Wikimedia Commons: https://commons.wikimedia.org/wiki/File:Great_Wall_of_China_in_Beijing_(210069864438).jpg

41 Wang Hui (王翙), CC BY-SA 4.0 <https://creativecommons.org/licenses/by-sa/4.0>, via Wikimedia Commons: https://commons.wikimedia.org/wiki/File:E_Huang_and_N%C3%BC_Ying.jpg

42 Cleveland Museum of Art, CC0, via Wikimedia Commons: https://commons.wikimedia.org/wiki/File:Unknown_artist_-_Rank_Badge_with_Single_Crane_Motif_-_2019.78.1_-_Cleveland_Museum_of_Art.jpg

43 Silentpilot, CC0, via Wikimedia Commons: https://commons.wikimedia.org/wiki/File:Red-lantern-1202514.jpg

44 https://commons.wikimedia.org/wiki/File:Lion_dance2015.jpg

45 Zeimusu assumed (based on copyright claims)., CC BY-SA 3.0 <http://creativecommons.org/licenses/by-sa/3.0/>, via Wikimedia Commons: https://commons.wikimedia.org/wiki/File:Rabbit_in_the_moon_standing_by_pot.png

www.ingramcontent.com/pod-product-compliance
Lightning Source LLC
Chambersburg PA
CBHW050335010526
44119CB00004B/151